Louis I. Kahn

Louis I. Kahn
by Vincent Scully, Jr.

George Braziller   New York 1962

Contents

"One feels the work of another in transcendence—in an aura of commonness and in the Belief"　　　KAHN, 1961

It has seemed proper for this preliminary study to concentrate upon Kahn's buildings and projects and to treat his architectural theory as it interprets those works or can itself be interpreted through them. Kahn is therefore allowed to speak for himself at the rear of the book, where two of his major statements of principle and method, one of 1955, the other of 1960, appear in full.

In my *Modern Architecture* and elsewhere I have attempted to state Kahn's position in relation to the history of architecture as a whole. Such general considerations are not absent here, but they are not normally in the foreground. The attempt is to focus directly upon Kahn himself, which it is a privilege to be able to do. Interpretation, as noted above, is necessary, but the facts are more essential still, because no book has hitherto been written about Kahn and the numerous articles that exist are fragmentary and often inaccurate, through no fault of their authors, because of previous lack of data. Extensive chronological lists of biographical events and buildings have therefore been appended, as well as a substantially complete bibliography. Errors and omissions may still be found in them, but they have made use of Kahn's records and personal recollections as well as of all other available sources. They have taken shape largely through the efforts of individuals other than myself. Much material for them was gathered by Thomas R. Vreeland, Jr., of Philadelphia, a graduate of Yale, who was employed in Kahn's office for a number of years, and they have been completed and rearranged under my direction by Robert A. M. Stern, a graduate student at Yale, whose developing study of the life and times of George Howe, a close associate of Kahn's, has aided me immeasurably in this book. I am also indebted for much help to Marshall Meyers of Kahn's staff, a former editor of *Perspecta*, to Miss Helen Chillman of the Yale Art Library, and to Richard Wurman and various other members of Kahn's office and of his Master's Class at the University of Pennsylvania. To the students of architecture at Yale, who have since 1952 been faithfully publishing Kahn's work in their journal, *Perspecta*, goes my heartfelt appreciation, as will, I think, posterity's. I am most of all grateful to Kahn, as they are, for the years I have known him, for what he has taught me about the inexhaustibility of man, and for the questions his work has forced me to pose.

There are no footnotes; references made in the text are all cited in the bibliography.

New Haven, March, 1962　　　　　　　　　　　　　　V.S.

Ten years ago Louis I. Kahn, then over fifty, had built almost nothing and was known to few people other than his associates in Philadelphia and his students at Yale. None of them would at that time have called him great, although his students generally felt, with some uneasiness, that he should have been, even might have been, so. But within ten years the "might-have-been" has turned to "is," and Kahn's achievement of a single decade now places him unquestionably first in professional importance among living American architects. His theory, like his practice, has been acclaimed as the most creative, no less than the most deeply felt, of any architect's today. He is the one architect whom almost all others admire, and his reputation is international. European critics have even insisted—so claiming Kahn as once they claimed Wright—that he has been seriously underrated at home.

To begin to understand Kahn requires a major intellectual effort, and indeed it ultimately involves the rewriting of contemporary architectural history. A generation brought up on Hitchcock's and Johnson's *International Style*, of 1932, or even Giedion's *Space, Time and Architecture*, of 1941, could hardly hope to perceive Kahn's quality at once. Nor could he, more importantly, have been able to find himself easily in it. From this observation, one of the major factors contributing to Kahn's lack of significant production during the thirties and forties comes to light. Kahn was, in large part, a part of that academic education, centered upon the French *École des Beaux-Arts* and called in America, generically, *Beaux-Arts*, whose later phases many historians of modern architecture, including myself, had so long regarded as bankrupt of ideas. In a formal, symbolic, and sociological sense the *Beaux-Arts* probably was bankrupt by the early 20th century, not least in the 1920's in America. But the researches of Banham and, more recently, of Stern, now force us to recognize the tenacious solidity of much of its academic theory, as distilled from Viollet-le-Duc and others by Choisy, Guadet, and Moore. That theory insisted upon a masonry architecture of palpable mass and weight wherein clearly defined and ordered spaces were to be formed and characterized by the structural solids themselves (plates 5, 6). One of the earliest extant drawings by Kahn, a student project of 1924, shows that he learned that lesson well—apparently better, as a comparison could demonstrate, than the other students of his time (plate 7). Kahn's characteristic difficulty with the skin of his building, with, that is, the element which seemed to him neither structure nor space, is equally apparent in a comparison with other contemporary projects as, for example, with that by William

Wurster, published at the same time. Kahn was also trained
in the Beaux-Arts manner to regard the buildings of the past
as friends rather than as enemies, friends from whom one was
expected, perhaps with more intimacy than understanding,
to borrow freely.

So trained, Kahn emerged during the late twenties into an
architectural world where his lessons were not valued, neither
by most Beaux-Arts designers (by whom, especially in
America, the structural rather than the eclectic side of the
theory was normally honored in the breach) nor by the
livelier, more creative, and apparently iconoclastic architects
of the Modern Movement. Soon called "The International
Style," the new architecture of the twenties and thirties generally concentrated upon lightness, maximum thinness in the
solids, and fluid spaces, usually defined not by the structural
skeleton but by non-structural planes and skins of wall. In this
world Kahn was never at home, and two decades of his life
were given over to a not entirely successful attempt to find
a place within it. So his few buildings and his drawings of
the thirties and most of the forties often hardly seem to be
from his hand, whereas his European sketches of 1928 and
his perspective of the Richards Medical Research Building,
of 1958–60, are clearly by the same man, one who can again
create the forms to which he is instinctively drawn, his pencil
constructing the two in an obviously related way (plates 1, 2).
The later drawing is tauter and more articulate as to parts.
It is that of a practiced constructor and a modern architect,
but it also shows that Kahn could now use what he had originally been trained to see and to do. He had come into his
inheritance.

The road back, and forward, began to open out for Kahn
about 1950–52. That renewal also owed much to the pervasive
influence of Le Corbusier and to a new direction taken by the
Modern Movement as a whole during those years. But in the
end the richness of theory and practice which Kahn has since
poured forth stems intrinsically from the character of his own
genius and from the life he has lived.

Kahn's father, now a lean and erect man of ninety, was a
craftsman in stained glass and a sergeant in the Imperial
Russian Army. His mother, who died only in 1958, was a
harpist. While still a very small boy, Kahn was badly seared
when the apron in which he was carrying hot coals from the
communal fire flared up in his face. In 1905 the family emi-
grated from the Baltic island of Osel to Philadelphia, where
they lived in profound poverty. Kahn's upbringing was wholly
Jewish, though not strictly Orthodox, but as a boy he discovered and read the New Testament on his own. He has since

12   said it was as if a sword had pierced him. "They've got us," he said, and buried it in the snow.

The immigrant's son was gifted in every imaginable way, most of all as musician and painter. After winning a number of scholarships he finally settled upon architecture as a career, though he probably could have been a concert pianist. (He has said that there was no space in his room for both bed and piano so he slept on the piano.) Later, when asked to define a city, Kahn was to say, "A city is a place where a small boy, as he walks through it, may see something that will tell him what he wants to do his whole life." Philadelphia was such a place for Kahn. In the early 20th century it shared character- istics with many other large cities in America but was alive with a special intensity of its own. Beneath it lay William Penn's special dream of brotherhood and his gently lucid plan (plate 3). In the early 19th century the city, by then the cradle of American liberty, was one of the most urbane in the United States. By the later 19th century its row houses and Classic Revival monuments had been supplemented or supplanted by an urban design of new scale and unprece- dented, almost savage, force (plate 4). It was to the work of Furness that Louis Sullivan of Boston responded in the early seventies, and from that time onward the most forward-looking architecture of Philadelphia was characterized by bold plastic invention and uncompromising toughness. Wilson Eyre, one of the most important architects of the Shingle Style, built in and around the city, somewhat taming the exuberance of the earlier generation and simplifying its forms. The Beaux-Arts architects of the early 20th century carried the process fur- ther, though still usually retaining something of the special Philadelphia flavor, but the town itself, like most American cities, was slowly escaping from their new avenues (plate 120A), and indeed from all architectural control, as its popu- lation swelled, its slums darkened, its suburbs proliferated, its arteries choked and decayed.

In 1920, however, the Architecture School of the University of Pennsylvania was conceded to be the most successful Beaux-Arts institution in the country. Its guiding light was Paul P. Cret, who had trained at the French École and settled in Philadelphia in 1905. Kahn has always regarded Cret as his master. "I had good teachers," he has said, and, like Cret, the young Kahn did not regard himself as a revolutionary. As a dutiful student he traced and adapted forms from the archetypal academic books: Letarouilly, D'Espouy, Guadet. Underneath such direct eclecticism, the history and theory of architecture were taught more or less after the method of Choisy (plates 5, 6). The general effect upon Kahn has al- ready been described (plate 7). The spaces of his student drawing are symmetrically made by solid structure and distinguished as to type by changes in the structural scale. Some of the rigidity of plan concomitant to that attitude (which was parallel to, though not the same as, the Beaux-Arts predilection for classicizing symmetry) has also tended to remain constant in Kahn's design. Kahn has since said that he was less affected at the time by Choisy's *Histoire*, since he could not read it, than he was by the flashier plates in some of the books noted above. Yet the plan types drawn by Choisy for Rome reappear in Kahn's mature work, while his structural axonometrics of Greek temples look forward to the piece by piece pre-cast concrete construction of Kahn's greatest buildings. But for that mature synthesis to occur in Kahn's work, other experiences had to intervene.

After graduation in 1924 Kahn, then employed by Molitor, the city architect, was put in charge of design for the Philadelphia Sesquicentennial Exhibition of 1926. The plan, largely Kahn's by default, was pure Beaux-Arts Baroque and of small interest, as were the buildings. Kahn clearly was given the job because he was the best renderer in Philadelphia, almost as dramatic as, though less brutal than, the redoubtable Hugh Ferriss (plate 8).

In 1928 Oscar Stonorov arrived in Philadelphia. Through that modern architect Kahn first became aware of the Modern Movement as such and of Le Corbusier's writing, which, he says, he loved from the start. But when he visited Europe in 1928 (on money saved from overtime work on the Sesquicentennial), he saw none of that architect's work, though he did visit his classmate, Norman N. Rice, then working for Le Corbusier and apparently the first American to do so. Edward Stone and Louis Skidmore were in Europe at the same time. Kahn himself was drawn to Greek and Roman antiquity, especially to Paestum, where the Temple of Athena challenges the Italian hills and the two temples of Hera weigh heavily upon the plain (plate 24). In the fifties Kahn was to say: "Consider the great event in architecture when the walls parted and columns became," but his early drawings of Paestum cannot now be found. He loved the Italian Romanesque as well, and his sketches of Siena and San Gimignano have been preserved, both constructed from the bottom up of strong flat strokes with the side of a carpenter's pencil (plates 1, 9). So broad are the horizontal bands at San Gimignano, not present in the building itself (nor in Louis Skidmore's drawing done at the same time), that Kahn's tower curiously prefigures that of the Philadelphia Saving Fund Society, built in 1930–32 by George Howe and William Lescaze (plate 11). Kahn was to meet Howe himself in 1930, and their friendship lasted until Howe's death in 1955. In 1931 some of Kahn's sketches were published in an article on drawing he wrote for *T-Square Club Journal*, an architectural magazine supported by Howe (plate 1). This is Kahn's first published statement, and some of his theory of the specificity of things, to be developed in the fifties, is already apparent in it. "We must learn how a steamboat is to be given its character," he writes, "or how a New York business building is seen with an absolute detachment and devotion equal to that awakened by a cathedral."

Upon his return to Philadelphia in 1928 Kahn entered Cret's office and worked with others upon the drawings for the Chicago Centennial of 1933 and the Folger Library of 1929–32 (plate 10). The latter is a good indication of the limits to Beaux-Arts invention at that period: no actual integration of structure and space in practice; a simplified classicism of mass and detail (but the interior Jacobean); a certain imposing vacuity of expression. Later in the thirties such a formula was to serve Nazi and Soviet obscurantist purposes ideally. George Howe broke with this mode, philosophically as well as formally, in his great Philadelphia bank and office tower (plate 11). Certain elements from that skyscraper, such as the exposed columns and cantilevered floor levels, were to appear in Kahn's work later, but Kahn does not admit to conscious influence from Howe's design of any period.

With the Philadelphia Saving Fund Society Building the Modern Movement came to Philadelphia, and with it the Great Depression of the thirties. Cret's office dwindled; others disappeared. There was literally no work to do anywhere. Kahn was often on relief. He tried his best to find jobs or at least to keep himself busy, as the appended list shows. Most touching and important of all was his association with the Architectural Research Group, made up of unemployed architects and engineers. His design for a projected rebuilding of a slum block, of 1933, already shows his grasp of the new idiom of modern architecture and of contemporary European planning methods (plate 13B).

In 1937 Kahn was able to complete a commission on his own, the Ahavath Israel Synagogue, in Philadelphia (plate 12). This building was nothing to be ashamed of. A shell of brick wrapped around two sides, that where the adjacent buildings were contiguous and that, elegantly perforated (the notice board is not Kahn's), behind the decisive terrace on the street. On the other side, where an areaway provided some space, Kahn stopped the brick and set large simple windows in a stuccoed wall with its own separate flat cornice. The intersection could hardly be more awkward or, prefiguring Kahn's later work, more correct in terms of the function each wall is serving.

The brute courage necessary to keep one's self-respect alive

during much of that decade can hardly be imagined now, but
through its trials Kahn was forced into a consideration of the
role of architecture in modern life as he could never have
been by the Beaux-Arts. Significantly, *T-Square Club Journal*
became *Shelter* and was dominated by Buckminster Fuller.
The group housing projects with which Kahn was associated
made him wrestle with the hard demands of purely functional
planning (plate 13A). Characteristically, he was later to perceive the special beauty implicit in such demands. These sup-
plied the element of life as lived which had been lacking in
his academic training, and they required Kahn to think, as he
was thenceforward always to do, of architecture as the construction of the human environment entire, of the city as a
whole. Philadelphia was clearly a major center of such conceptions in the thirties, and Catherine Bauer, who wrote her
classic study of housing in 1934, knew Stonorov, Alfred
Kastner, and Kahn well. Indeed, the first federally sponsored
housing project, Juniata Park, was built in Philadelphia in
1934, designed by Alfred Kastner in association with W. Pope
Barney. In such projects economy permitted only modern
architecture, in the narrowest sense of that term, to be built
(plate 13C). And it was in these years, Kahn has said, that
he came to revere Walter Gropius the man and the apostle
of sociological responsibility, though not especially his buildings. One was alone with the problem, the cinder block, and
the two-by-four at that period, and one's noble friends across
time, once so childishly intimate, were now remote; they
would have to be faced again, if ever, as man to man. To that
end Kahn *read*, as he had not done before. Le Corbusier's
books were especially important to him, and later he was to
recall that experience. "I came to live in a beautiful city
called Le Corbusier," he said.

In 1941 Kahn entered into association with George Howe,
and in 1942 Stonorov joined them. David P. Wisdom, who has
been with Kahn ever since, entered the firm as a draftsman.
Howe soon left the office to take up his duties in Washington
as Supervisor of Building; but his name remained connected
with the firm for some time. Howe, Stonorov and Kahn's
Carver Court was one of the best housing developments built
during the war years, but only the supporting masonry walls
of the raised units in any way prefigure Kahn's later work
(plate 14). In 1944 Kahn published an article entitled
"Monumentality." During the following decade such themes
were to proliferate, reiterating the need felt by a deprived
generation for grander architectural expression. Significantly,
Kahn's was among the first. In it he characteristically concentrated upon structural possibilities but was still involved in
the International Style aesthetic of maximum lightness and so

16　proposed structures of welded steel tubing. In attempting to deal with a mode fundamentally unsympathetic to him, he turned rather desperately back to Choisy and to the latter's drawings of Gothic architecture, for which he had not cared much in the twenties (plate 15). His own drawings recall those of Le Corbusier, which he apparently often traced in these years, and which themselves owed more to Choisy than either those of the Beaux-Arts as a whole or Kahn's own earlier sketches had done. Kahn was thus making fresh contact with the most useful side of his education through the influence of the most potent modern architect, and he himself dates his deep personal interest in Choisy from this time. His eventual integration of the wiry linearity characteristic of Choisy and Le Corbusier alike with the massive shadows of his earlier style can be seen in a comparison between the drawings discussed earlier (plates 1, 2, 5, 6).

In 1947, with the departure of Richard Bennett from Yale, and upon the recommendation of that remarkable man, Kahn was hired as Visiting Critic and soon became Chief Critic of Design. Personal recollections are that he talked a good deal about structure (directing, in 1949, a collaborative project in which he required that the building form result from "unconcealed structure"), sketched quickly and expressively with that black pencil, but had as yet no consistent approach to design. The impression was of deep warmth and force, compact physical strength, a printless, cat-like walk, glistening Tartar's eyes—only bright blue—a disordered aureole of whitening hair, once red: black suit, loose tie, pencil-sized cigar. It was at this time that he began to unfold into the rather unearthly beauty and command of a Phoenix risen from the fire. Earlier he had looked as fey as Harpo Marx. Much later he gave up smoking and bought a gray suit.

The years 1947–50 were a period of transition for Yale and for many other architectural schools no less than for Kahn. There was unmitigated intellectual chaos and little post-war building to do. But the academic atmosphere was good for Kahn; he had after all been brought up in it. While he developed as a teacher, in which role he was much beloved, his design began to clarify itself and to become more fully his own. Such is apparent in his Weiss House of 1948–49 (plates 16, 17A, B). The plan seems to derive from the contemporary "Bi-nuclear" schemes of Marcel Breuer, but in Kahn's hands it takes on a new, square-cut decision. Utilities are grouped in the (then) Bauhaus-Harvard manner, and in this the functional though not yet the structural germ of Kahn's later "service spaces" may just possibly be sensed. The masonry and plank and beam structure is clearly articulated (a word often used at that period), and one feels Kahn's love

for the character of every stone and board. In some details, 17
and in feeling, the Weiss House resembles the ideal farm proposed by Paul and Percival Goodman in their agrarian-radical
planning polemic, *Communitas*, of 1947. The plan of the
Genel House of 1949 is of rather less interest, and too many
elements may confuse the whole. But the walls and passages
around the garden terrace are a sketch in miniature of the
archaic world of Kahn's ultimate desire and of his drawings
of long before (plates 1, 18).

In 1949 Kahn got a chance at a larger building on his
own. He and Stonorov had made drawings earlier for an addition to the Philadelphia Psychiatric Hospital, but nothing had
been built. In 1949–50 Kahn carried out the Bernard S.
Pincus Therapeutic Building (plate 19). Here he used the
same movable plywood panels in double-height windows that
he had employed in the Weiss House (plate 17A). The wide-
span structure, carried outside the walls on the tubular lally
columns which were ubiquitous in those years, was of light
steel open-work joists. This was the very last time that Kahn
was to make use of metal construction in any form. Henceforth
he was to design only in reinforced concrete and masonry,
even when he thereby eventually lost commissions which by
their very natures called for spanning with steel. He was soon,
in other words, to understand and to have confidence once
again in his own structural and formal predilections and his
original training.

The main addition to the Hospital, the Samuel Radbill
Building, was thus carried out in concrete, designed in mid-
1950, finished by 1953 (plate 20). Its regularly spaced columns, its taut surface, and its brick towers recall both Mies
van der Rohe at I. I. T. and Alvar Aalto at M. I. T. (plates
26, 27), and they look forward to Kahn's later work of the
fifties. The rather inconsequential canopy which tells us where
the entrance lies derives from some of Le Corbusier's forms,
but its grouping of three columns prefigures Kahn's own Synagogue Project of 1954. The sunshades of hollow tiles are
rather like Le Corbusier's in feeling but entirely Kahn's in
conception. The Psychiatric Hospital is thus a collection of
fairly disparate elements which were to be integrated with
each other later, and it shows that Kahn was beginning to
sense his way and to reach out to new statements of modern
order and structural force.

In 1950–51 other decisive events occurred. This academic
year was spent by Kahn at the American Academy in Rome.
That institution had been the proudest jewel of the American
Beaux-Arts in its salad days. It had been founded in 1896,
largely through the efforts of Charles Follen McKim, who
was eventually able to elicit the financial support of J. P.

18 Morgan for the project. To it had come several generations of Prix de Rome winners; and architects, painters, sculptors, writers, musicians, classicists, archaeologists, and art historians had all dined in varying degrees of hostility around its single long refectory table. In its early years the Academy had clearly encouraged the kind of picturesquely archaeological design which had eventually squeezed out Sullivan and Wright and against which the Modern Movement as a whole had so firmly reacted. It therefore was, with some justice, a favorite whipping boy for that movement's historians. By 1950, under the directorship of Laurance Roberts, the climate had changed. Its artists were all creatively modern artists, and its resident archaeologist, Frank E. Brown, had a wide knowledge of all architectural history and welcomed nothing so much as a fresh idea or work of art. Antiquity so came alive for those members of the Academy who had the wit to see it, and for Kahn it must have been as if a rather baggy mistress, abandoned in the bread lines, had walked youthful into the room. His sketches around the Mediterranean show the great masses of Egypt looming, the columns of Karnak (plate 21), the quarries at Aswan. The buttressed wall of the Athenian Acropolis rises (plate 22), and the tholos at Marmaria lies before Apollo's throne (plate 23). Most of all, though no adequate drawing remains, the columns still stood at Paestum, and Kahn saw them once again (plate 24). Arcuated Praeneste, the foliating Palatine, and, especially, the miraculous spaces of Hadrian's Villa at Tivoli (plate 25) were all seen anew with an intensity of vision the Beaux-Arts had never been able to summon up.

This was the case partly because a great architect and lover of the Mediterranean, Le Corbusier, had himself learned by this time how to embody its noble masses in modern constructions and programs. Kahn visited Le Corbusier's *Unité d'Habitation* at Marseilles while it was under construction and where, as early publications of the building had already stated, the columns of Paestum stood in their contemporary form (plate 28). Soon these were to be joined by the Maisons Jaoul, first published as drawings in 1952, where a more vernacular idiom of substantial concrete lintels and solid brick walls was to be seen (plate 29). Even before leaving America, Kahn, as his Psychiatric Hospital showed, had also been aware of Alvar Aalto's dormitory at M. I. T. (plate 27), with its strong brick masses, directly functional stair housing, and aggressive corner towers. (Kahn just missed that most splendid of all lectures, given by Aalto at Yale in 1947, when he drew the Acropolis of Athens on the blackboard and said, "In Finland in the reconstruction we shall build no temporary buildings, because not by temporary building comes Parthenon on Acropolis." Later Kahn was to say much the same thing to his expediency-minded building committees at Trenton.) Not massive, but equally expressive in a structural sense, were Mies van der Rohe's new buildings at I. I. T., where a precisely joined fabric of steel and brick defined static volumes of space with classic authority (plate 26). In all these events the generally non-structural, thin wall-planed, rather pictorial phase of the twenties and thirties was being brought to a close and the principles of modern architecture were, in that sense, approaching those which Kahn had learned from the Beaux-Arts.

So, too, in the same sense, was the Yale Department of Architecture to which Kahn returned in 1951. Concentration upon the integrally jointed wooden frame—calling to mind Kahn's later use of pre-cast concrete components—played an increasing part in its doctrine during 1950–55, largely through the influence of Eugene Nalle, then critic of first-year design. In this he was supported by George Howe who, in part through the efforts of Kahn, had become Chairman in 1950 and remained such until 1954. His successor, Paul Schweikher, held similar ideas. Along with the frame went an insistence upon its structural definition of single or separate volumes of space rather than upon the earlier, spatially fluid, fundamentally non-structural type of International Style planning. Here, too, Kahn's later work is recalled, but he avoided the several anti-intellectualisms in which Yale's movement temporarily foundered, and must instead have been reminded anew of the traditional method of Choisy. At Yale Kahn was also in close contact with Philip Johnson and with that architect's then very fresh principles of classicizing order. More broadly, the debilitating hostility between architect and historian which had characterized some of the pedagogy of the Modern Movement was on the wane at Yale, despite periodic attempts to revive it, and Kahn was exposed there to free, as against what might be called court (late Beaux-Arts or Bauhaus) Art History in general. He often dropped in on lectures; San Gimignano, Hadrian's Villa, and the work of Brunelleschi were rather obsessive favorites at the time.

The English architects, Peter and Alison Smithson, had already come to much the same point, and for much the same reasons. Their Hunstanton School of 1951–53, the first monument of the English "New Brutalism," was based upon a toughening of Mies, and they ascribed its intrinsic symmetry to Renaissance and, by extension academic, precedent as well, citing Wittkower's *Architectural Principles in the Age of Humanism*, of 1949, as their authority. Later the Brutalists, like

20 Kahn himself, were to be more permanently influenced by the Maisons Jaoul.

Yet it was the late work of Mies which had the most immediate effect upon American architects in the early fifties, and it is Mies one thinks of in the first phases of Kahn's design for the Yale University Art Gallery and Design Center, of 1951–53 (plates 30B, 32). Kahn received the commission for this crucial building, the first modern one at Yale, through Howe's persuasive influence. The project, an addition to the old art gallery, was required to accommodate for some years almost two floors of architects and a basement of graphic designers, as well as gallery exhibition space and offices. Eventually the whole was to become gallery, as it will do when Paul Rudolph's Art and Architecture Building is completed across the street. Thus it was almost impossible to design specifically for this program. All any architect could do was to make spaces which were as large and uncluttered as possible in order to allow for maximum flexibility and openness. Consequently, the decision to design the floors as simple open lofts was not itself a Miesian one but was related to that architect's general practice, as was the clear rectangular envelope in which they were contained and the precise linear detailing of its window walls.

These were the original decisions; after them the resemblance to Mies abruptly ceases, but they did create the building's exterior shape. This Kahn fitted into its site with admirable sensitivity, complementing the older buildings and terminating their sequence with authority. He enhanced, where he might easily have destroyed, the several levels of Weir Court to the north (plate 30A). On the west the glass should clearly have been recessed to the inner plane of the piers (plate 32) but the wall of brick on the busy street to the south, its floor levels indicated by string courses, was the only possible solution on that side and created a façade which seemed at first brutal to some but has since been appreciated for its severe urbanity, worthy of Italy (plates 31, 32). This quality was more complete before the gray paving blocks in front of the building were idiotically removed some years later and grass was planted in their stead. The latter has, appropriately, refused to grow in that place. Kahn may have been right when he later said at Yale, "The paving block is the grass of the city."

Inside, much else occurred. Early in the design Kahn gathered the circulation and utilities together in a rectangular space through the center of the building (plate 33). Part of this section was a circular stair tower with splendidly diagonal flights within it (plate 36). He then made drawings for a series of concrete vaults, carried on beams, which were to span the major spaces from east to west (plate 31). The design wavered between this and other schemes until Buckminster Fuller, Kahn's old acquaintance from *Shelter*, came to Yale in 1952 and talked incessantly for some weeks (plate 34). Out of this traumatic event grew one of Fuller's great-circle domes (triangular, spherical structures), built of cardboard by dazed students and placed on Weir Hall tower, where it rotted impressively for some time. Kahn sometimes admits, sometimes denies, that all this affected him; but the fact remains that the final, post-Fuller scheme for the Art Gallery's span was now conceived by him as a concrete space frame, made up of tetrahedronal elements and poured in place (plates 33, 35). The design was modified by the consulting engineer, Henry A. Pfisterer, because of the problems of shear involved in the small sections at the points where the tetrahedrons joined. It became a braced beam system, but the visual effect remained more or less tetrahedronal. Since the slab for each floor was poured across the apices of those shapes a continuous horizontal void resulted, through which Kahn ran channels and ducts for flexible lighting and ventilation from the central service core. The mechanical equipment was now an integral part of the building's hollow fabric.

The columns were kept as few as possible, in line with the impossibly flexible program, and this Kahn was later bitterly to regret. Movable "pogo panels" were designed so that many works of art could be displayed, isolated or with others, while still allowing the main volume of space and structure to remain clear (plates 37, 38). The final effect of the interior as a whole, despite its vicissitudes, was of uncompromised integrity and force. All the old words out of Gothic Revival architectural criticism were recalled by it: honesty, reality, masculinity; and it was praised in this way by a host of admirers from contractors to deans. The concrete was left rough with the marks of its forms upon it, as Le Corbusier had already treated that material, but Kahn's shapes were crystalline, not muscular. The massive, repetitive, mathematically insistent canopy of the ceiling thus set off the specific works of art below it as, in my opinion, no white plane of plaster could have done. Their dense and luminous embodiments of human action were now tested by a forceful environment with its own physical order counter to theirs; and, as the Greeks well understood, their special qualities and meanings were enhanced thereby. The analogy is not strained, since we largely construct the settings for our actions and our works of art; the Greeks chose natural ones of special authority (plate 22). In that sense Kahn, as in later buildings, was constructing a landscape, "ageless and unwearied," physically expressive of Law. But so well did he create the flexibility desired by his clients that a later gallery regime—impelled, ironically enough, by that preference of the thirties for weightless planes and pristine hermeticism (Museum of Modern Art) which Kahn had by now outgrown—was able to mutilate the interior considerably by throwing out the pogo panels and sheathing over most of the columns and concrete block walls. This event might be considered of small importance, since some day it will obviously be rectified (the building can carry its scars, a witness for it) except for the fact that it gave added impetus to Kahn's thinking about how the spaces should have been ordered and constructed so that what they "wanted to be" might have been made so clear that alterations would have been inconceivable. He recognized, for example, that the pre-conceived rectangular plan and column placement had never been brought into accord with the triangular order of the spanning tetrahedrons.

Kahn had been talking about Order for some years, first in terms of small crystals, and his developing thoughts of the mid-fifties about *Order* and *Design* were published in *Perspecta* in 1955 and are reprinted at the back of this book. They state his thinking of that period better than I could paraphrase it here. He soon came to believe that in allowing himself to create a single wide span with few columns in the Art Gallery he had shown inadequate recognition of the Order intrinsic to the problem, and in *Perspecta, 4*, of 1957, he published a lyrical essay on "the thoughtful making of spaces," in which the column figured largely: "A column should still be regarded as a great event in the making of space. Too often it appears as but a post or prop." In 1952–53, directly after the Art Gallery, the column had already begun to figure for Kahn in the highrise towers of his Mill Creek I Housing Project for Philadelphia (plate 39). There they recalled those of the Philadelphia Saving Fund Society Building (plate 11), while the column-like corner articulations of the low blocks can remind us of Hugo Haering's housing at the Vienna Werkbund of 1932, published by Bauer in 1934. (Mill Creek I was concurrent with a beautiful planning scheme for the city of Philadelphia which will be discussed later with Kahn's subsequent developments from it.) This first project as built was still not Kahn entirely mature, though the space defined on the plateau between the low houses and the towers is as splendid as anything imagined earlier at the Beaux-Arts for exiled Balkan monarchs. But in the project for the Adath Jeshurun Synagogue in Elkins Park, of 1954, which would have stood fairly close to Wright's later "mountain of light," the column began to come fully into its own (plates 40, 41). It was grouped in touching clusters on a triangular plan to house the stairs, support the roof, flourish

behind the rabbi, and create small spaces at the sides and a
grand space in the center. Kahn said, "It is what the space
wants to be. A place to assemble under a tree." He might also
have said: "for ten men or a thousand."

The synagogue was published in *Perspecta, 3,* as were the
Adler and DeVore house projects of the same year (plates
42–44). In these, each unit of space was made by its own
integral column and spanning system in which space for the
mechanical equipment was also provided. The demanding
reality of the fabric, already felt in the Art Gallery, was now
complete; the spaces were the result of an order intrinsic to
the thing constructed. The environment in which men live was
thus thought of not as a simple extension of the human whim
but as having an Order of its own and so as being part of a
larger order of things. Subjective desire and objective reality
were balanced. Space, as in the late work of Wright, the developed International Style, and some contemporary criticism,
was no longer to be the whole determinant for Kahn. Nor, as
for example in the work of the eminently Beaux-Arts architect,
Perret, was structure alone to dominate. Instead, Kahn was
to attempt an integral union of space and mass, solid and
void. He was seeking a truly classic wholeness of being. Such
constituted a set of recognitions, related to those taught at the
Beaux-Arts, which had passed far beyond that institution's
concept and practice toward a state more basic and complete.
The houses were not constructed, but Philip Johnson, as others
have already pointed out, was reminded by them of Schinkel
and freely adapted their scheme for his highly successful
Boissonnas House, designed in 1955–56.

If the columns and spanning members so come alive to
make the space, what of the wall? That such was now a diffi-
cult problem for Kahn can be seen in his A. F. of L. Medical
Service Plan Building in Philadelphia of 1954–56 (plates
45, 46). Indeed, the columns of that building were something
of a problem as well, because, except for a few major areas,
they do not actually define most of the spaces. The conception
was still partial, and can be experienced only in the two-
storied lobby, where the crudely designed Vierendeel trusses
demand that the structure of the building be considered. How
to clad such a massive frame? Kahn finally drew a kind of
cellophane envelope over the whole, with the aggressive structure standing threateningly inside it at the lower floors. Kahn
was already implicitly refusing to design those elements which
he could not yet wholly rationalize in terms of an intrinsic
order of being. He called such designing "pattern making,"
and although he could do it, and sometimes wanted to do it,
he usually would not do it from this time on.

It is therefore apparent that Kahn, by 1955, had worked

24 himself back to a point where he could begin to design architecture afresh, literally from the ground up, accepting no preconceptions, fashions, or habits of design without questioning them profoundly. That "great event," so rare and precious in human history, when things were about to begin anew almost as if no things had ever been before, was on the way. On the other hand, memory would eventually play an important part in the process, most richly and intensely for Kahn; but it would come only when the first major steps to liberate the mind for it had been taken. First would come a naïveté of vision which most men can never achieve and only the most intelligent can imagine to be possible. Nothing would be taken for granted. (Even though Kahn was to say to the editor of *Perspecta, 7*, "I have the usual artful fainting spells, you know.") Every question would be asked: What is a space, a wall, a window, a drain? How does a building begin? How end? Every expedient dodge and avoidance well known to the dullest student in second-year design was henceforward normally to be impossible for Kahn. He was beginning where almost nobody ever gets to be: at the beginning.

It is possible that in modern architectural history before Kahn only Frank Lloyd Wright ever began so wholly at the beginning. Elsewhere I have tried to show that an extremely close parallel exists between Wright's works of 1902–6 and Kahn's of 1955–60. I shall therefore refer to but not stress that relationship here. It should only be pointed out that anything of the kind has been wholly unconscious on Kahn's part. He has said that he was never consciously influenced by Wright, and I do believe him in this. Again, such makes the parallel all the more significant; perhaps it indicates a general pattern that occurs when the problem of architecture is studied afresh by a mind which intends to know the whole. Secondly, Wright and Kahn have occupied rather similar historical moments and have functioned in the same way in them. Both, that is, began their invention—Wright early in life, Kahn late—at a moment when the general architectural movement was toward clear geometric order: in the forties and fifties late Mies and Johnson, in the eighties and nineties Richardson, Sullivan, Burnham, and McKim. In the nineties most architects soon came to conceive of such order in the usual Picturesque-Eclectic terms, and the movement as a whole turned into neo-Baroque formalism, overtly eclectic, overtly decorative. Wright conceived of order in intrinsic terms and rebuilt architecture from the ground up with it. In the fifties—after Mies—some of Johnson's work, almost all of Stone's, Yamasaki's, and others has followed the first course, the neo-Baroque, decorative one. Kahn has followed the second: Wright's course. The first course heralded, in the nineties, the end of something; in the late fifties it would seem to have been doing the same. The impression becomes inescapable that in Kahn, as once in Wright, architecture began anew.

With Kahn, as with Wright, the germinal project was cross-axial in plan. This was the Bath House for the Trenton Community Center, of 1955–56, part of a larger general layout (plates 47–51). But where Wright interwove the axes of his Gale and Willitts Houses for spatial continuity, Kahn keeps each of his four spaces uncompromised by giving it a separate roof cap, with oculus, of its own. The volume-defining hipped roofs recall those used by Wright in his Hillside Home School, of 1902 (plate 52). Kahn's do not project in Wright's overhang, keeping instead to their contained volumes, but in both cases they are supported by massive piers. Wright's piers were solid, Kahn's hollow. "Today we must build with hollow stones," Kahn said in 1957, and the reason is clear; to house the services, as these do here. Indeed Wright was to use hollow piers housing utilities in his Unity Church of 1906 (plate 87). So Kahn said, "The nature of space is further characterized by the minor spaces that serve it. Storage rooms, service rooms and cubicles must not be partitioned areas of a single space structure, they must be given their own structure." Here they are in the piers (plates 48, 50). Except for these, the space order which results recalls that of Brunelleschi at the very beginning of the Renaissance. The fluid continuities of Wright's late-19th-century perception have become the static squares and circles of a Vitruvian ideal (plate 49). Perhaps the Beaux-Arts had been able to produce a son who could eventually begin again at what was fundamentally its own beginning; and here reference should be made back to Kahn's student project of 1924 (plate 7). Yet the Bath House could not have achieved the archaic force it possesses if the Modern Movement had never occurred and the housing projects of the thirties and forties had not been built. Here the material of the piers is neither Beaux-Arts limestone or modeled plaster nor Wright's agrarian Wisconsin masonry; it is cheap concrete block used straight, the mortar smeared across it, so acquiring its own severe and noble scale in terms of mid-twentieth-century economic and technological realities.

Kahn's struggle with the various building committees at Trenton in regard to such realities was apparently a nightmare. The Center as a whole was never built by Kahn and passed through other architects' hands later. In his several schemes Kahn tried to develop for this extensive structure the principle he had so lucidly stated in the small Bath House (plates 53, 55, 56). Grouped masonry columns were used to define the service spaces. Wright had done the same in his cross-axial Martin House of 1904 (plate 54). But in Kahn's

26 building the piers rose high in mighty companies and were connected in fours by heavy arches. Each group, forming the major spaces, supported its own pre-cast concrete roof cap, which made each unit of space volumetrically distinct from all others. Where a wide span was necessary the rather unsatisfactory solution of carrying a number of such roof caps on concrete beams was adopted. Kahn was insisting upon his unit instead of upon what the required larger spaces "wanted to be" in their own terms, though at one point he did envisage some huge hoods for the purpose. Later schemes were rather less successful, since Kahn was clearly having trouble with the big spaces. The reason seems clear: he was determined that the pressure of the fabric would always be closely felt. Unlike Wright he did not want sweep. Yet his unbuilt complex here is one of the major losses to contemporary architecture (plate 56). It would have made a splendid northern landscape supremely welcome in New Jersey: in the flat fields a forest, somber, shot through with lighted glades.

It should be stressed that Kahn still had very little work to do. He remained poor. In 1956 he entered the competition for a library at Washington University in St. Louis. Here he tried to develop the cross shape he had used at Trenton with a forest of columns and an essentially pyramidal massing (plates 57, 58). The whole was a toughly jointed thicket, permeated with light in section and sheathed in a variety of ways on its exterior surfaces. One may perhaps feel that the order of shape and structure was again taking over unduly from the order of spaces and that Kahn could not yet conceive of integral structural and spatial units of a scale appropriate to the functions of so large a project. It was about this time that architects were saying that Kahn, whom they now deeply respected, was designing the ugliest buildings in the world. ("But I love them," one said.) Kahn was answering criticism by saying that "Order does not imply beauty"; he was clearly looking for something more than skin deep, and his search for intrinsic order is dogged at this period. His Research Institute for Glenn Martin, in study during 1955–57, again sought out the order of the cross axis and its structure (plate 59). Here the cross in plan tended once more to build toward the pyramidal in elevation. The order of spaces finally unfolded with exact symmetry in units which were constructed of two massive piers placed slightly nearer the center than the thirds of the space, with roof slabs cantilevered off them. There is considerable rigidity in the conception still, but it was apparently a revelation for Kahn's students at Penn, who saw it, for the first time in their experience, as a lucid demonstration of Order unfolding.

In 1957 the problems began to resolve themselves. That

such coincided with Kahn's departure from Yale was Yale's loss and a gain for the University of Pennsylvania, which acquired one of the greatest buildings of modern times.

It is, I suppose, appropriate that such should have occurred there. Philadelphia was Kahn's home as New Haven had never been; it was his urban place, the center of his practice and of his architectural imagination in the larger problems of civic design. For it Kahn had already done much planning work and had advanced several imaginative urban schemes which will be discussed as a whole later. In relation to them he had proposed by 1957 two related tower projects. The first, of 1952–53, was a light pre-cast concrete space-frame extended in elevation, a surprisingly thin web for Kahn but explicable in terms of his Fuller space-frame phase already referred to (plate 60). The second, of 1957, with which Anne G. Tyng was associated, was a triangulated structure of concrete elements which took on the bodily force of a column, now bracing itself diagonally (plates 61–63). "A vertical truss against the wind," Kahn wrote in *Perspecta, 4,* ". . . in contrast with the accepted many-storied trabeated construction corrected for wind." He was thinking specifically of the Seagram Building, "a beautiful bronze lady in hidden corsets." Kahn's columns group on their piazza like those of the earlier Synagogue project, but now men were to be involved with them as they rose in the building's many off-set and interlocked levels. At the major intersections great knuckles gathered (plate 62), recalling Kahn's earlier statement in *Perspecta, 2,* "If we were to train ourselves to draw as we build, from the bottom up, when we do, stopping our pencil to make a mark at the joints of pouring or erecting, ornament would grow out of our love for the expression of method." The plaza below was designed for parking and services in line with Kahn's statement "that a street wants to be a building equally organized as to space and structure as any other piece of architecture" (*Perspecta, 4*).

In 1957 Kahn was already settled at Pennsylvania. There he became closely associated with two remarkable engineers: one, Robert Le Ricolais, a uniquely poetic visionary and theorist; the other, August E. Komendant, an outstanding practitioner and authority on pre-cast, pre-stressed concrete. Le Ricolais had lectured on "topology" earlier at Yale, and following his topological vocabulary Kahn now began to substitute the word *Form* for his earlier word *Order,* so giving rise to certain terminological ambiguities that can best be explored later. Kahn could not have found two more sympathetic engineers, one for theory, the other for practice, and Dr. Komendant, who after this was employed as a teacher by the University, was his structural consultant for the Richards

28 Medical Laboratories at the University of Pennsylvania (plates 64–74). Their structure was to affect for good the techniques of the whole concrete pre-casting industry from the factory to the site. Design began in 1957 and construction was complete in 1961. The adjacent Biology Building was designed at the same time and is now being built. The Medical Laboratories have been extensively published and were the subject of an exhibition at the Museum of Modern Art, which produced an excellent Bulletin devoted to them.

Kahn's first conception was that the service towers should act as columns, but when it was pointed out to him that the floors could be more effectively cantilevered from their thirds, the columns were added at those points. He has been criticized for the visual ambiguity between the big towers and the comparatively slender columns, which are actually doing the structural work. It can only be pointed out that a less scrupulous architect would have avoided the difficulty by ignoring his engineers and beefing up the slab to compensate for its uneconomical bearing. The early sketches show arcuated beams between the towers, diminishing toward the corners. These were a prefiguration of shapes Kahn was to use in later buildings, but as basic fabrication methods made their demands felt they were eliminated. The towers, too, housing stairs and exhaust and intake ducts for the laboratories, were originally of much more elaborate form, some circular like the stairs of the Yale Art Gallery, others ribbed and with various elaborate terminations (plate 64). For a long time they cantilevered out in a series of projecting stages, so expressing alike their non-bearing character and the greater number of ducts rising through their upper levels (plate 65). This feature, too, slowly disappeared in the interests of directness and economy, until the concrete, brick-clad shafts achieved their present strictly rectangular form, reminiscent surely of San Gimignano and Siena but hardly arrived at through any simple Picturesque-Eclectic process (plate 71). Kahn was beginning to find his family of forms in his own decently realistic way.

The columns rise alongside the towers in a clearly jointed dry structure of pre-cast units (plate 67). Between the two columns on each side of the square they define run massive concrete beams, poured in place. Interlocked with these are pre-cast open concrete joists, one to each sixth of the structure. The point where they reach the spandrel beam is clearly visible on the exterior, and beyond them that beam is thinner to the corner, since it is doing less work (plate 70). In earlier designs the cross joists were two instead of one in each bay, but through Komendant's calculations and for reasons of further economy, the second was eliminated. In the Biology

Building further calculations have eliminated the other cross
joist by thickening the slab (plates 2, 66). Such will com-
plicate construction procedure, but as seen in the elevation
drawing, the units will be fewer and will seem bolder, also
reflecting, as Kahn has said, his sudden perception that the
crane was merely an extension of the arm and that any unit
it could lift should therefore become the governing one. Like
a Gothic architect, Kahn welcomes the change, as, like a
Gothic building, his own is a triumph of skeletal order.

Brick spandrels are carried on the beams, and they and
the glass are set tight up to the front plane of the structure
(plate 70); Kahn was still refusing to fiddle with the skin
when it could not yet be wholly conceived of by him in terms
of the structural and spatial order. He has since paid for this
—though restrictions in the budget also had something to do
with the problem—in the aluminum foil and other unpleasant
devices the scientists have resorted to in order to cut down
the sun's heat and glare, which is inadequately controlled by
the blue-tinted glass panels under the beams. Kahn's building
has also suffered, a bit like the Yale Art Gallery, from the
flexibility of floor level which the structural system provides.
That is to say, each level "wants to be" one space and would
be noble beyond belief if so (plate 73). This can be tested
today only at the entrance (plates 68, 69), where the spandrels gape shark-like at the corners, the stairs spilled out
below them, and the great open lobby stretches out into one
of the few tragically grand spaces constructed in the modern
world. (Such seems not inappropriate, since the human de-
termination to best nature in order to stay alive in the teeth
of the facts must probably come to be perceived as tragic in
the classic meaning of the word; otherwise its murderous
self-preservation is only embarrassing.) At best, the floors
could have been divided into four laboratories at the beams,
since the structure is cross-axial; at worst seven (plates 66,
67). Yet even this would have left, in terms of utility, the
laboratories generally too small and too much area for circulation. At present the laboratories are mostly what Kahn
himself has elsewhere called grab bags of space, divided at
will by their occupants, often ignoring the structure as ex-
pediency dictates and spilling out into the halls. Nor are the
utilities all in the towers; some are housed in the central
mass and snake out to the laboratories in bewildering profu-
sion. The service-served concept of spaces has clearly not
achieved an integrated state.

Despite all this, in any one of the laboratories, with the
solemn structure interwoven with utilities just above one's
head, it is clear that this is a place that exists and makes demands of its own (plates 72, 73)—a salutary reminder for

30   men. One also often looks, in that cluster of glazed towers, out of one's own laboratory into others, where other men are engaged in similar activities. It is a classic town, the true polis of common action, not just San Gimignano but the modern brotherhood of work. Dr. Jonas Salk was later to recognize that quality in it.

The Biology Building will have an open portico running right through at ground level, and its library carrels—"A man with a book goes to the light," Kahn had written earlier—will project forward of the taut envelope as deeply perforated walls at the upper floor (plates 66C, 74). In earlier schemes they were part of a true library, two stories high and lower down. Now they will create a kind of terminating cornice or attic in the new section, but in the first one Kahn had already answered several of the questions asked earlier: How does a building begin? How end? His answer in a sense had been that it need do neither. The glazing of the lower laboratories appears out of the ground and the highest has merely a gravel stop above it; in the Biology Building the topmost spandrel beam will be higher, so forming an integral pre-cast parapet against the sky. The towers rise beyond, "a crown of towers," and are terminated only by the gesture of those whose tops are rent (plate 70). It is the only open gesture in a structure which otherwise is everywhere crystalline and taut.

The building is entirely successful as seen on its site: a majestic spread from the present garden to the south (plate 71); an urbane sequence of towers from the footpath on the north (plate 2); a mighty assertion from the north-south walkway that approaches it through the dormitory court on that side. This last characteristic is in accord with some of Philadelphia's most typical earlier forms. One thinks especially of Furness (plate 4), although Kahn has said, I believe correctly, that he was never personally drawn to that architect's buildings. Yet a common rude strength is surely theirs. Neither Furness nor Kahn employs Wright's engulfing and soothing continuities of space, and this is the point at which the Medical Building diverges formally and philosophically from the Larkin Building, to which its service towers, columns, and interwoven spandrels must otherwise be closely compared (plates 75, 76). Wright in 1903–4 manipulated the structure itself to create a spatial release from its tensions; Kahn in 1957–61 envisaged no such release. Again one is led to conclude that the central theme for Wright is psychic comfort; for Kahn, challenge. Wright, early in the century, deals in the optimism of expanding possibility; Kahn, toward its middle, in the severity of fate.

Kahn seems to have fully experienced no building by Wright until 1959 when, sadly enough after the latter's death, he was taken to see the Johnson Wax Building and, to the depths of his soul, was overwhelmed.

By the late fifties commissions began to come to Kahn in large numbers, until he was swamped with work. His project for the Morris House, of 1958 (plate 77), is superficially closest to the Richards Laboratories and also recalls Wright, in this case the latter's Richard Lloyd Jones House of 1929. Both buildings have the ambiguity of scale that seems inherent in unrelievedly vertical piers and planes at domestic size, and both were the result of experiments with those structural and spatial modules which dominated their designers' thinking of the moment. The Tribune Review Publishing Building, of 1959–61, recalls the Morris project in its vertical piers (plate 79) and Le Corbusier remotely in the sculptural force of its side elevation, where the blocky cooling tower shakes itself loose from the sheathed spaces on both sides of it (plate 78). Yet the window treatment here is purely Kahn's, and it is a prototype for that in much of his later work. In it the wall, with which, as noted earlier, Kahn had always experienced some major difficulties, now began to function for him in terms of light. Its non-bearing brick screen is cut by wide openings above eye level, with slots below, thereby flooding the interior with light but cutting the actual glare. The structure permits this, based as it is on a simple plan with a longitudinal spine which rises the full two-story height, carries the services, and divides the high interior space in two, so separating the quiet work areas from the printing-press side (plate 81). Pre-stressed concrete beams span from this to piers of solid concrete brick, and there glazing is set between them (plate 79). Below, planes of wall contiguous to the piers reduce the glass to a vertical slit while, above, a pre-cast concrete sunshade forms an integral cornice (plate 80). Kahn has generally been an architect of the flat site, but here the building adjusts to the change of level, lowering where the ground falls away but civil on the street (plates 78, 79), though the front entrance walk gives pause.

Mill Creek Housing II, of 1959–62, built directly below the earlier towers (plate 39), again recalls Le Corbusier at a certain remove, here most specifically the Maisons Jaoul (plates 29, 82). Like Stirling at Ham Common earlier and Rudolph in his Married Students' Housing at Yale later, Kahn was clearly impressed by the fundamental vernacular of brick and concrete suggested in those crucial buildings. Cost requirements in terms of American building techniques limited the integrity of the conception for Kahn as for Rudolph, and the pre-cast plate with its entrance canopy is here mainly a visual element, not the projection of a beam, and it is therefore appropriately treated in thin planes. The walls are

32 bearing, but the construction within is the usual builder's welter of studs, two-by-tens, bridging, strap hangers, and so on. Nevertheless, the long blocks of dwellings, as grouped externally, make a good Philadelphia row house neighborhood, the white plates gesturing up the slope, the most "unpatterned" window mullions arresting with the directness of vernacular gaucherie. In the Community Center for Mill Creek, on the other hand, the size of the spans permitted a true brick pier and pre-cast concrete beam construction, so that the detailing of the exterior, with its projected massive piers dry-capped, is an integral expression of the order with which the units are fitted together (plates 83–85). It should be noted that all pieces are separate and are laid up like masonry blocks or heavy wooden beams. Again, as always in structure as in space, Kahn prefers to avoid continuities, and one is referred once more to the drawings of Choisy (plate 5). Inside, the major spaces consist of large, high, square bays that are spanned and wholly formed by pinwheels of four interlocked beams. Outside, as within, their supporting piers are clearly distinguished from the enclosing walls, though the slots which were to have revealed the former to the interior were omitted in construction (plates 83, 85). The bolts that hold the beams together are left visible, and a pre-cast lantern rises in the central smaller square they define, so becoming an important element of the exterior massing. The fine hard red brick of Philadelphia and the factory-finished white beams are set off by a ceiling of gray concrete blocks, hollow and prestressed as "Dox" plank. These now common industrial units recall Wright's reinforced block spans of the twenties and create a rather disquieting effect of what-holds-them-up until one gets used to it. Again, we are forced to be aware of the fabric's realities and so required to accept the objective existence of things outside the self. The building as a whole is, in any event, a direct demonstration of Kahn's "meaningful order of spaces and structure." It will be observed that there are no really wide spans in it; the bay proportions are almost Vitruvian. When a wide span is inevitable Kahn has had certain difficulties, and such arose at Rochester.

The First Unitarian Church at Rochester, now under construction, is most of all a demonstration of Kahn's sequence of what he now calls Form and Design (plates 88–91). For Kahn Form is immaterial, almost Platonic in its implications, ideal. He has called it "dream-inspired," and the time of "belief" in it the time "to begin." Nature is Form, but it is not aware of Form, does not conceive of Form. Such conception is possible only to man, because he alone has a sense of "wonder." This last sounds Aristotelian, and its humanism replaces Kahn's earlier tendency to speak of form "growing,"

as in nature. Form is now the result of an ability to envisage
fundamental configuration and order: in an architectural
sense the general shape that the program under consideration
"wants" to assume. Consequently, Form is not simply "function" for Kahn, but a conceived Order; thus a being, if as yet
immaterial. At Rochester, in this sense, Kahn's first plan was
almost like his first pure Form drawing, the meeting hall in
the center, the school and services around it (plate 88). It is
clear that for Kahn Form is Symmetry, as it was for the
Romans. Can we say that in a practical sense Kahn's Form is
actually his Beaux-Arts background and his early preferences,
which, however, he has now learned how to use wholly afresh?
Because now comes Design, "the maker that serves belief."
Through Design, Form is made material. In this process what
the building largely "wants to be" as an ideal scheme is profoundly modified by how it can be built and, perhaps most
of all, by what all its specific functions "want to be." Perhaps
we can therefore say that one part of Design for Kahn derives
from the functionalism of the thirties, profoundly intensified
by structural demands and by the fact that he desperately
wants to be told everything about possible uses for various
areas so that he can derive "meaningful" new shapes from the
functional processes themselves. He does not sentimentalize
those processes but uses them as a way toward articulate
specificity and, beyond that, to new visions of Order.

This seems a fair description of Kahn's method; it is surely
a more realistic one in terms of how the human mind actually
seems to work than the random flow-pattern and area studies
that pass for a pragmatic way to form in some quarters. True
enough, Kahn's terminology can create some confusion, since
"form" is normally used to describe the materialized work
of art itself. Yet for an artist, concerned less with the finished
thing—which by that time is after all no longer his—than
with the miracle of conception, the use of "form" to describe
such conception seems entirely reasonable. So Kahn names
with the big, round word that state of the work which seems
most essential to him. At the same time, Kahn's process can
surely work in two ways: also, that is, from Design leading
back to conceptions of Form, as he has said. Thus the sequence
is from the immaterial to the material and back to the immaterial—to, that is, "transcendence" in the end. Again, such
appears to be a reasonable description of an artistic process
and of the ultimately transcendent character of any work of
art, which is never the sum of its parts or a simple record
of the intentions behind it. Yet Kahn's buildings tend to indi-
cate that his major direction in any project is, in his own
terms, Form—Design: from what is first imaged, really out
of what the human mind already knows, to what is then step

34   by step felt for, hammered out, and so re-imagined. Philip Johnson had advanced a rather similar concept, though with less emphasis on the later steps, in a symposium with Kahn and others published in *Perspecta, 2.*

So at Rochester Design brings Form materially alive. The entrance lobby, the library, the women's workroom, and the stairs want spaces differing from those of the classrooms, and they get them (plate 89); but what might be called the psychic presence of the original Form is always felt, so linking the specific to a general Order. Then comes Light, and through it the wall now becomes wholly, three-dimensionally, alive. It does so, typically, through Kahn's unappeasably wondering consideration of its most intense meaning for the interior spaces: to admit light to them and to shelter them from light. So at Rochester the walls go deep back to give the windows glare-dimming reveals, and step out to provide window-seat spaces, lighted from the sides. The whole wall, inside and out, is plastic with light, with what a window "wants to be." At the same time, its expression is deeply structural, a buttressed mass (plates 22, 89). Above the exterior walls rise the four hoods pulled back above the corners of the central meeting space and scooping out its hollow with light (plate 90). They took position there after many other schemes were tried, in all of which Kahn had attempted, as noted in other projects, to articulate the main span into several spatial units. Now four columns support two cross beams from which the ceiling slabs gently lift toward the voids formed by the hoods, placed where they are partly because they are more easily supported near the corners (plate 91). Kahn's structural isometric here, done from below in hard lines, again recalls Choisy (plate 5). Wright's Unity Church of 1906 is also recalled in the fortress-like exterior, the crossed beams and the top light (plates 86, 87), but at Rochester the spaces are entirely different, again separate from each other rather than interwoven, and the units of·structure have become large in size. Wright, for continuity, uses interwoven overhangs; Kahn, to define, in contrast, a sharp-edged mass, has designed terra-cotta copings for his walls.

Much the same process of Form and Design can be felt in Kahn's Goldenberg House project of 1959 (plates 92–94). He has described how he felt it first as a symmetrical cube. Then the functions kept trying to push out of the cube to find their own free shapes, but the cube tried to hold them in with its linear discipline. Finally Kahn discovered that he could frame them diagonally and hold them to Order that way. So seen, the folded planes of the house are wholly alive around the purely square void of its central court, from whose corners the framing diagonals radiate, as if tying back the

outward-thrusting spaces but drawn upward by them toward
the light. The complex intersections in plan and massing are
thus not picturesque but wholly expressive of two systems of
formulation: the will to be general and the will to be specific;
to be ideal, and material.

Kahn's house for a single person in Chestnut Hill, of 1959–
61, seems much more conventional (plates 95, 96). It is a
simple cube with timber spans, a tough and blocky mass, split
through the center by its circulation area. The wide windows
above with slots below recall those of the Goldenberg project,
but here they are proportioned with more active force. The
opening wooden panels in them are of the Le Corbusier type,
as is the two-storied, balconied living room and, from an
earlier era, the stucco finish on the masonry walls. The spat-
tered windows of the kitchen side are functionally placed but
also suggest both Le Corbusier and the English Brutalists.

In the Fleisher House project of 1959 Kahn's sense of
space, structure, and light opened up the round arch for him
once more (plates 97, 98). The plan, unlike that of the
Goldenberg project though in study at the same time, remains
basically symmetrical, because here it is purely the space-
structural Order which suggests and finally dominates the
Design. These are spatial units, made of bearing masonry
walls with pre-cast arched caps set upon them. Some of the
arches are glazed, others bricked, some open. The rectangular
walls rise higher than eye height, though sometimes cut into
by small voids for view, and a taut volume of air and light
expands above them. Le Corbusier's vaulted projects of the
fifties are recalled, but most of all the Mediterranean tradition
behind them, as the arches touch lightly upon their supports,
seemingly held up, like some of Hadrian's, by the very atmosphere they define. The rounded void with a slot below can
also be found at Roman Ostia, visited by Kahn in 1950.

Light again had much to do with Kahn's project for the
American Consulate at Luanda, in Portuguese Angola, and
caused the wall to take a further step into space (plates 99–
103). Here one has the feeling that the project has otherwise
remained fairly close to the first Form stage—perhaps appropriately so in this official program. The residence and
consulate are both rigidly symmetrical, but the spaces are
organized lucidly within their blocks (plates 100, 101).
Pierced masonry piers outside them carry huge pre-cast beams
which support a sun roof of heat-breaking tiles, entirely separate from the unbroken rain roof below (plates 101, 102)
and so recalling Paul Rudolph's project for Amman, of 1954–
55. Next to the piers, in front of all the floor-to-ceiling windows,
free-standing walls, cut with their own arched voids and slots
like tremendous keyholes, break the shattering glare of the

place (plate 103). Kahn has explained how such walls seem to cut glare better than pierced screens do and at the same time permit one to look out. He might also have said that their effect is spatial and massive rather than cosmetic, like that of the thin screens used by Stone and others. The openings in such walls need no glazing; they can exploit the rare purity of solid and void. "So therefore," wrote Kahn in *Perspecta, 7,* "I thought of the beauty of ruins . . . the absence of frames . . . of things which nothing lives behind . . . and so I thought of wrapping ruins around buildings." The wall now takes on added layers in space and memory. One thinks again of Rome, but the planes are stiffly propped above their reflecting pools; it is a two-dimensional Rome, not a three.

Kahn's Town Hall for Bristol, Pennsylvania, at present in the planning stage, is also a clearly Roman scheme (plate 104), but as the plans of the Salk Institute for Biological Studies take shape it begins to appear that this ambitious project will constitute Kahn's most complete and integrated work to date (plates 105–114). Dr. Jonas Salk, having visited the Richards Laboratories, felt that Kahn was the only architect who could give him what he wanted: a place where scientists engaged in pure research could work in an environment consonant with the larger humanistic meaning of what they did. He liked the Richards towers, but got a low building himself, and understood the point of that in terms of his site and his functional requirements.

The program resolved itself into three main divisions: laboratories, a common meeting house, and housing. The original site, running directly to the cliffs above the Pacific, was more extensive than the present one. Kahn's preliminary presentation, of early 1960, consisted of laboratory towers, something like those at Pennsylvania, near the road, housing scattered in a loose arc farther in, and finally an extensive Meeting House, like a palatial expansion of the Fleisher project, above the cliff. The site was then perforce restricted, split by a deep ravine which thinned it down from its widest portion to a narrow saddle which culminated in a high bluff, now looking toward the sea over the coastal cliffs. Kahn's later scheme, at present (March, 1962) getting into working drawings, admirably uses the shape of the place: flat laboratories on the wide plateau, dwellings in a taut contour arc along the edge of the ravine, the Meeting House filling the top of the bluff and reached only by a sweep of road along the saddle (plates 105–107). The dwellings, connected by a single walkway along the height, are still under design. The laboratory has achieved its final state and the Meeting House practically so.

In the laboratories the vertical ducts of the Richards Building have been turned on their sides, housed in the hollows of

spanning box girders and vented from huge hoods at the flanks
of the building (plates 108, 109, 111). The pre-cast units of
structure have thus continued to become larger as the crane
can lift them. Order, once an affair of repetitive crystals for
Kahn, is now felt in grand components, space-making themselves. The folded cross-spanning sections are in the depth of
the girders, the lower one high enough to walk through, and
all utilities are now directly channeled through the structure,
sent down to the lower story, up to the second. The laboratories themselves occupy the entirely open spaces created by
the mighty beams. Entrance to them is through the columns,
once splayed to their footing (plate 108), now rectangular
(plate 111). Here structure, "served" spaces, and "servant"
spaces are entirely integrated, so resolving the conflicts apparent in the Richards Building; and this "meaningful order"
was almost instantly arrived at in Kahn's design.

Not so in the studies between the laboratories; their problem demanded a more complicated sequence of Form and
Design, and its solution was again characteristic of Kahn.
Early shapes used were pure derivations from the fanning
pattern of the lower peristyle of Domitian's palace on the
Palatine or from the "Teatro Marittimo" of Hadrian's Villa
(plates 25, 108). It will be recalled that Wright had long
before adapted the plan of the Villa as a whole for his Florida
Southern College of 1939, and had used shapes from or related to it in later projects, while Le Corbusier had supplemented his sculptural Hellenic impulses with a series of drawings of the Villa's spaces which culminated in his top-lit
megara at Ronchamp. More directly, the shapes used by Kahn
can be found not only in Choisy (plate 6) but also infinitely
repeated in the composite photostat of Giovanni Battista
Piranesi's maps of Rome, drawn by him for his book on the
Campus Martius, probably of 1762, which now hangs in front
of Kahn's desk (plate 115). Nervi, too, has used this curvi-
linear pattern in some of his ribbed slabs. Kahn had intended
to support the studies on columns which arose from the associated garden at the lower level to grasp them about at the
thirds of their arcs (plate 108); but a further stage of Design
intervened: the scientists could not see the sea from these
shapes. Thus they were modified and the present simpler
forms grew out of them (plates 105, 111).

Patterns from Rome and, most particularly, from Ancient
Rome as imagined by Piranesi at the very beginning of the
modern age, have played a part in the process at the Meeting
House as well (plates 110, 112-115). (An early sketch had
been traced by a draftsman, partly as a joke, from a plan
of one of the units of Hadrian's Villa itself. "That's it," said
Kahn.) The major fountain splashes within a colonnade partly

38   untrabeated, a ruin. Rounded shapes, to be found again and
again in the Piranesi plan, and contrasting with the austere
court inside, now push out from the main mass, recalling the
splendid follies of 18th-century gardens but mightier than
they: Walls "that nothing lives behind," shielding the glazed
spaces from glare. They are to be constructed of poured concrete, reinforced and calculated, like the squat piers of the
laboratories, against earthquake tremor. Because Dr. Salk felt
that stone would be more soothing to the eye than concrete,
Kahn sheathed them (and they will remain so at Salk's request
if the money holds out) in soft yellow-brown Cordova sand-
stone from Texas, full of fossil crustaceans and more ambigu-
ous biological forms. Kahn used the thin sheets of this stone in
a special way, however, since he left spaces between them ap-
proximately where the reinforcing tenses the concrete (plate
114). It is a classic system of wall articulation, rationalized
in new structural terms. Here, through his own process, Kahn
goes beyond the flat planes of Luanda to an expression the
Beaux-Arts had never quite attained: that of an integral
Rome, with a noble wall of cladded concrete, voluminous,
generous, and arched, behind which Hadrian himself would
have felt at home to ponder the complex structure of life.
What, after all, is the question biologists ask, but Hadrian's,
that begins:

> *Animula vagula blandula*
> *Hospes comesque corporis . . .*

Again a parallel with Wright comes to mind, in which
Kahn has compressed two or three decades of Wright's career
into a few years. That is, Wright's work from 1902 to 1906,
despite the formative influences upon it from the Shingle
Style, Japan, and so on, was almost pure invention in terms
of reintegration, thus a true beginning. So also Kahn's from
1955 to 1959. From 1914 onward, Wright seems to have welcomed memory more and more and to have incorporated its
shapes more obviously in his work: Mayan in the teens and
twenties, finally, by the late thirties, Rome and its antecedents.
So now Kahn in 1962. It is probably no accident that both
turned to Hadrian, since that haunted Emperor was perhaps
one of the first, certainly one of the most conspicuous, men in
Western history for whom—all ways having opened, which
more true than another?—conscious, selective memory was a
major determinant of life.

Is this a pervasive problem of the modern world—all possible, nothing wholly serving, no way the only Way, memory
all too free to choose? If so, does such inevitably prevent a
direct view of present problems and so limit creative capacity
or divert it toward easy eclecticism? It cannot be said to have

done so for Hadrian himself, or for either Wright or Kahn.
It is true that it eventually tended to direct Wright away from his earliest integration of structure and space toward configurations more purely space-dominated, often constructed as might be, but it also liberated and enriched his overweening desire for continuous spaces more and more. So too Kahn has gained in spatial command, where he has most needed to gain, but his structural concern has not faltered. If he can advance along that line, toward integration, not away from it—keeping, can one say, the "dream" and the "reality" in balance, the present and the past in his hands—he may yet endow his age with an image of wholeness matched only by Wright's and Le Corbusier's and so most rare in it up to now. Such rarity should not be considered surprising, insofar as it is linked to that rarest of human gifts, the instinct for how and what to remember.

Kahn would thus seem to have found a way to accomplish what neither the architects of the Beaux-Arts nor the more impatient formalists of this decade had been able to do: to make the past and the present—the continuum of life—one, in terms of reason no less than wonder. Past and present do now play as one in his art. To watch him struggle with a problem is to see this. The dormitories for Bryn Mawr, now under study, show it. At present they are close to pure Form: three cubes touching at the corners, advanced and recessed walls creating side lights, a general rigid symmetry (plate 117). He has only begun. Now he wants to know how the use of each space can show him how to Design it; he harasses his assistants to study each functional requirement to that end. Unlike most architects, he will henceforward hang breathless upon specific client demands, the more specific the better. Any one of them may cause him to redesign the building as a whole, which he will do if, in his phrase, "the Form does not hold." To help him he also has by his desk an unlikely 19th-century history of Scottish castles, in which a thick wall honeycombed with spaces of every conceivable shape caught his eye (plate 116). Circles and triangles, evidences of specific use, fragments of Form.

In 1961 Kahn designed a barge which sailed up and down the English Thames all summer and from which the American Wind Symphony of Pittsburgh played and fireworks were shot off at appropriate intervals (plate 118). He liked being listed on the accompanying program as "Barge Architect." Originally, the barge's canopy was to have been an inflated membrane of some sort, and plastic-impregnated cloth balloons formed the structural and spatial motif in Kahn's project of the same year for a General Motors Building at the New York

40 World's Fair of 1964 (plate 119). As in Le Corbusier's Phillips Pavilion at Brussels, of 1958, various images were to have been projected upon the interior surfaces which here, however, all expand, pinched at the neck like paper bags prepared by a boy for bursting.

One of the most important facts about Kahn is his pervasive concern for planning and civic design. Architecture does not stop or even begin for him with individual buildings but comprises the human environment as a whole. In this concern he is one with the great architects of all times and most specifically with those whose heritage was humanistic and who, like Le Corbusier but unlike Wright, held the city to be the ultimate work of human art. Kahn, with them, regards the city as a product of Form and Design, a complex of memory and action, with an Order of boundary and definition, not an animal sprawl. Philadelphia is Kahn's city, where as "a small boy walking through it" he found "what he wanted to do his whole life." The appended lists show his many associations over the decades with city and federal planning groups. He was Consultant Architect for the Philadelphia City Planning Commission from 1946 to 1954. Toward the end of that period he suffered a major defeat but produced a project which will probably not be forgotten in the future. His City Hall scheme of 1952–53 has already been discussed (plate 60). How far it might have gone is hard to say, but it was beaten by finances from the beginning. "It was too large," he has since said, "it should have been two." Along with it went a new traffic scheme for the center of Philadelphia of a realism and beauty unmatched in contemporary planning (plates 120A, B). Penn's streets, as well as those added later to his plan, were choked with automobiles; but in Kahn's scheme the automobile was neither to be thrown out nor to dominate. Expressways were to receive parking towers where the cars, parked, were to be out of sight, as a look at any parking lot can show that they must be, and other streets were to be designed as "go," "staccato," and "dock"—for fast movement, slow movement, or as harbors. Shopping streets would have no "go" traffic. Most would retain their buses or trolleys; others were to become pedestrian ways. The whole was meticulously worked out in a pattern intricate and complete. It was not a vision but a reasonable actuality in terms of all the facts but those, apparently, of political possibilities, and it should be contrasted with Kahn's rather offhand Voisin plot of 1941 to demolish all of Philadelphia. An integral monumentality could have resulted from the parking towers and Penn Center if designed under Kahn's hand (plate 121).

The scheme died, and Kahn soon left as Consultant but

continued to work over the plan on his own. In 1957 *Perspecta* published his developed tower project after the earlier City Hall space-frame idea (plates 61–63). Now the center of the city turned into splendor (plates 122–124). The monumental garages grouped close in, their towers, filled too with other functions, rose in pierced circular shapes of a multi-columnar structure—"stopping at the joints, making a line" —similar to that of Kahn's St. Louis library project of the same year (plate 58). A large Order began to be felt, not wholly a visionary one. In 1961 the Graham Foundation awarded Kahn a grant to develop his urban theme further, and this happily coincided with his reemployment by the City Planning Commission to study the redesign of the area called Market Street East. The interlocking projects are now (again, March, 1962) under study in Kahn's office (plates 125, 126, 128–130). Already a pattern has emerged, stroked in charcoal across the existing plan like Franz Kline's black images of active force (plates 125, 129).

At present, in this preliminary scheme, it is "Viaduct Architecture," the cars raised on long expressways which contain warehouses and so on beneath them and which lead to the Market Street center city area, now wholly enclosed as a built-up square by the viaducts and monumentalized by the great garages and shopping hemicycles (plates 126, 128). One of Kahn's old towers of 1957 abuts the Forum on the south side. The whole is beyond Rome, its scale large enough to subordinate, no less than to use, the motorcar. Water plays a part, flowing with the cars, since the northern viaduct is set with circular reservoirs, waiting to service fountains, as well as with triangular interchanges: again, fragments of Form, Piranesi's and Scottish, awaiting the chance to be Designed (plate 116). But the grand Form conception is there, giving the heart of the city what Kahn believes it most needs: a defining wall.

It would seem that Furness' old "Chinese Wall," itself a raised viaduct lined with buildings, which Kahn had hoped to raze in 1941 and which later planners did in fact demolish, has reappeared. Now, however, it is four walls instead of one and so purposefully defines the central area rather than simply dividing the city in half. It is no longer primarily a barrier but a maker of urban space.

Kahn's wall, with all its associated hemicycles, circles, water, and towers, can also be found in one of Viollet-le-Duc's drawings of Carcassonne, the medieval town restored by him and especially admired by Kahn (plate 127). In *Perspecta, 4,* Kahn had specifically recalled Carcassonne, describing one of his earlier Center City schemes:

42 Carcassonne was designed from an order of defense. A modern city will renew itself from its order concept of movement which is a defense against its destruction by the automobile.

Center City is a place to go to—not to go through.

Once more the question of past and present arises. Is Form, "dream-inspired," really Memory at the last? Is it in some way always pre-existent, a necessary stored pattern (fed by the experiences of the individual mind, not from a "collective unconscious") without which the transformations suggested by new particulars and fresh experiences have nothing to work upon, nowhere to begin, and so cannot create? It may be so for Kahn. It would appear to have been so for Wright and Le Corbusier, as what I have written about them elsewhere now seems to me to show. The memories of all three have eventually gone deep, and note should especially be taken of the fact that they are the strongest architects, not the weakest: the "Form-givers," as they have been called, not the Form-takers. One can envisage certain historical difficulties if the concept is carried far enough back in time, but such can undoubtedly be answered. It is probable that this is the way the mind creates, the way things come to be. One minor point seems clear: that to make anything in architecture, which has always been a large-hearted art, it is necessary to have loved something first.

Market Street East is clearly still in the realm of Form, of the broad conception of Order and of Burnham's "Make no little plans." Without this large frame of reference nothing meaningful can be done in the small. It now remains to be seen how Kahn, if given the opportunity, might Design specific buildings and spaces within the area and so conceive new forms thereby. He is now seeking out such in his most recent drawings (plates 129, 130). On Independence Mall, however, at the intersection of the proposed Greenway to the Delaware, Edmund Bacon, Executive Director of the Philadelphia City Planning Commission, has already made Kahn's projected Mikveh Israel Synagogue the pivotal building of an urban space where two long axes, one vehicular, the other pedestrian, will have their joining. Design for the Synagogue has only begun. It constitutes an opportunity for Kahn long due, long awaited, and an appropriate one, since this was the proud Sephardic congregation of Haym Salomon: patriot, partisan, spy, condemned to death for the Revolution and, totally unrecompensed, one of its major financiers to the utter limit of his personal fortune. A financial genius, he died in 1785, no richer than Kahn was born.

In his visits to the University of Virginia, for whose new Chemistry Building his drawings are well under way, Kahn sleeps in Stanford White's Colonnade Club, behind the intri-

cately articulated units of Jefferson's splendid Lawn. Above,
to the southeast, that same compelled and devoted intelligence
is physically palpable again in the house that surmounts the
dome of its little mountain. If Kahn's building continues the
general movement of his design, its brick walls and heroically
scaled members, no less than its structural integration of
"served" and "servant" spaces, should bring it closer in form
and intention to Jefferson's works at Charlottesville than any
of the buildings constructed there since that time. The University is to be congratulated upon the precision of its choice.

No one can sum up Louis I. Kahn. He is growing rapidly
and his present projects are subject to change without notice.
He has his limitations; his inherited reluctance to employ light
steel trusses and frames may be among them. But next year
he may have conceived the "meaningful order" of those as
well. Despite his growing use of arched forms, he has so far
fundamentally been an architect of separate structural components, of the column and lintel and the point load; thus he
prefers concrete pre-cast rather than poured, assembled piece
by piece and lovingly jointed. His buildings, despite their
Roman connotations, are hard and normally without covering
finishes; they are exactly what they seem: not for the faint-
hearted, which is as it should be. Kahn therefore requires wise
and courageous clients who are willing to forego the gloss of
superficial perfection in order to take part in a sustained and
demanding process of which they may one day be proud. His
schemes do not always come off; they can be uniquely awkward. There can be little doubt that this tendency is a necessary concomitant to their primal strength.

Historically, Kahn has already fulfilled his role. He has
shown, as Wright did earlier, that Order goes deep, is integral,
and can create inexhaustibly anew. He has done so according
to important mid-20th-century premises, imagining both a
total "order of being" and a tragic dignity in the environments
men construct. In this he is the perfect modern complement
to Le Corbusier, who has concentrated in his most monumental
buildings upon a sculptural embodiment of the human act itself. Kahn's humanism, his "symmetry," is not Hellenic like
Le Corbusier's, but, in the persistent American manner, rather
Italic, concerned primarily with interior space and its construction in terms of perceptible law. His buildings therefore
make "being" determinate—which is why he insists upon
both the "measurable" and the "immeasurable"—by pas-
sionately uniting the rational preoccupations of science with
the non-rational assertions of art and so convincing us emo-
tionally that they visibly embody the power of the facts: the
nature of things as they are. In the decade of what I have elsewhere referred to as the Late Baroque of the International

44 Style—in which Wright's late work was in its own way involved —Kahn has thus refound the beginning for himself and has shown what may be a general Way. Of that way he holds himself to be a primitive, as Cézanne did, but it links him with some of the broadest and soundest traditions of the architecture of the past, leading out from Rome, as Cézanne's did from Poussin. Perhaps most of all, Kahn has shown how to put to creative use what the mind can know, and has understood and written about that process of formulation more directly and humanely than any other contemporary architect.

As a teacher of the Master's Class at Pennsylvania, Kahn hopes to lead his students to define the problem for themselves, as he had learned to do. He can be maddeningly evasive as he tries to force them to think for themselves and to help him think. He offers no easy choices, there being in his view none such available in fact in human life, but only possibilities for action if they can determine where the critical fields of action lie. "The right thing done badly," he says, "is always greater than the wrong thing well done." Hence he earnestly seeks the good question, "better than the most brilliant answer," and learns from everyone. He does not pretend to be a master and wants no apprentices. People work for him like men in a grubby office on a busy corner in the heart of Philadelphia.

Kahn's architecture is *par excellence* the product of intelligence; it is fortunate for us all, not least for his city, that he has finally been able to link it with the things he loves. Yet a study of Kahn cannot help but show that his city is more than Philadelphia; he belongs to his profession as few men have done. Those American architects who revere him form a roster of diversity and distinction. The beginning of a special comradeship can be sensed among them, not, I think, a local school, but a more general movement, magnetized by Kahn. One recognizes a man. Kahn also tends to bridge the gap between the architect as artist and the architect as practitioner as no other seems able to do—just as he has been healing the breach between the present and the near no less than the distant past.

But how slow the growth of this tree, like an olive, bearing for the generations to come.

1901	Born February 20, Island of Osel, Russia. Parents: Leopold and Bertha (Mendelsohn) Kahn
1905	Brought to United States
1913–14	Won awards in drawing and painting. First prize, Wanamaker City Art Contest
1915	Naturalized citizen
1916–20	Student: Graphic Sketch Club, Fleisher Memorial Art School, Public Industrial Art School for drawing, carving and modeling
1919 and 1920	Awarded first prize for best drawings in high schools of Philadelphia, offered by Pennsylvania Academy of Fine Arts
1920–24	Student, University of Pennsylvania, School of Fine Arts. Awarded degree of Bachelor of Architecture
July 1921–Sept. 1921	Draftsman, Hoffman and Henon, architects, Philadelphia
June 1922–Sept. 1922	Draftsman, Hewitt and Ash, architects, Philadelphia
1923–24	Teaching Assistant, University of Pennsylvania
July 1924–June 1925	Senior Draftsman, office of John Molitor, City Architect, Philadelphia
July 1925–Oct. 1926	"Chief of Design" in charge of all drafting and design for all exposition buildings, Sesquicentennial Exposition, Philadelphia, John Molitor, architect
Nov. 1926–Mar. 1927	Worked on city planning studies, municipal buildings, office of John Molitor, City Architect, Philadelphia
April 1927–April 1928	Draftsman, office of William H. Lee, architect, Philadelphia
April 1928–April 1929	Traveled in Europe; did housing studies
1929	Exhibited paintings and drawings at the Pennsylvania Academy of Fine Arts
1929–30	Designer, office of Paul P. Cret, Philadelphia
1930	August 9, married Esther Virginia Israeli; daughter, Sue Ann, born March 30, 1940
	Exhibited paintings and drawings at the Pennsylvania Academy of Fine Arts
Dec. 1930–Feb. 1932	Designer with Zantzinger, Borie and Medary, architects, Philadelphia
Mar. 1932–Dec. 1933	Organizer and director of Architectural Research Group. Thirty unemployed architects and engineers studied Philadelphia housing conditions, planned housing projects, made city planning and slum clearance studies, investigated new construction methods, etc.
1933	Exhibited paintings and drawings at the Pennsylvania Academy of Fine Arts
Dec. 1933–Dec. 1935	Squad head in charge of Housing Studies, City Planning Commission, Walter Thomas, architect in charge, under W.P.A.
1934	Registered with the A.I.A. and began independent practice
June–July, 1936	Exhibition of Architecture in Government Housing, Museum of Modern Art, N.Y. Jersey Homesteads Project exhibited
1937	Consultant Architect for the Philadelphia Housing Authority
1939——	Consultant Architect for the U.S. Housing Authority
April 1941–Feb. 1942	Associated in practice with George Howe
1942–43	Associated in practice with George Howe and Oscar Stonorov
1946–52	Consultant architect for the Philadelphia City Planning Commission
1947–52	Chief Critic of Architectural Design at Yale University
1947–57	Professor of Architecture, Yale University
1948——	President, T-Square Club, Philadelphia

1950–51   Resident Architect, American Academy in Rome

1950	Invited by Government of Israel to be Architect Representative to the World Assembly of Engineers and Architects, Friends of Israel, to study Israel's Housing and Planning. Report. Trip sponsored by American Technion Society
1951–54	Consultant Architect, Philadelphia Redevelopment Authority
1953	Made a Fellow, American Institute of Architects. Cited for education
Feb.–June 1956	Albert Farwell Bemis Professor at School of Architecture and Planning, Massachusetts Institute of Technology
1957 to date	Professor of Architecture, University of Pennsylvania
1959	Delivered closing remarks, C.I.A.M. Tenth Congress, Otterlo, Holland
1960	Awarded Arnold Brunner Prize by National Institute of Arts and Letters
	Lecturer at Yale and Harvard, University of California, University of Houston, University of North Carolina, Tulane University; fellow at Princeton. Guest speaker for Southern California Chapter, A.I.A., Honor Awards Banquet
May 1960	Invited by Japanese Government to participate in World Design Conference, Tokyo
1961	Consultant Architect, Philadelphia City Planning Commission
	Awarded fellowship by Graham Foundation for Advanced Studies in the Fine Arts to pursue his investigation of larger aspects of civic design
1962	Lectured in Philadelphia, Ontario, and Chicago
March 14, 1962	Delivered Annual Discourse to the Royal Institute of British Architects, London, England
March 28, 1962	Received "1962 Philadelphia Art Alliance Medal for Achievement"

Chronological List of Buildings and Projects

Early Designs

1929–30	Worked on design for Chicago World's Fair buildings, and for buildings in Washington, D.C., and France, office of Paul P. Cret, Philadelphia, Pa.
1930–32	Worked on design for Department of Justice Building, Washington, D.C., office of Zantzinger, Borie, and Medary, Philadelphia, Pa.
1933	Slum block Reclamation Projects, as Designer with the Architectural Research Group, Philadelphia
1935–37	Ahavath Israel Synagogue, North Philadelphia, Pa.
	Jersey Homesteads Cooperative Development, Hightstown, New Jersey, reclamation project for the Resettlement Administration, Washington, D.C. (Assistant principal architect to Alfred Kastner, and co-designer)
1939	"The Rational City Plan," a part of the Houses and Housing exhibit of the Museum of Modern Art, New York. This exhibit was also shown at the Pennsylvania Academy of Fine Arts and the Art Alliance, Philadelphia, Pa.
1940	Residence for Jesse Oser, 688 Stetson Road, Melrose Park, Pa.

Howe and Kahn

1941–42	Pine Ford Acres Housing, Middletown, Pa., for the Harrisburg Housing Authority

Howe, Stonorov and Kahn

1941–43	Carver Court Housing Development (Howe, Stonorov and Kahn, Designers; Stonorov and Kahn, Architects), Coatesville, Pa., for the Federal Public Housing Authority
1942	Pennypack Housing, Philadelphia, Pa., for the Federal Public Housing Authority

Stanton Road Housing Development Project, Alley Dwelling Authority, Washington, D.C. (Project)

1943   Lincoln Road Housing Development Project, Coatesville, Pa., for the Federal Public Housing Authority

Stonorov and Kahn

1943   Lily Ponds Housing, Washington, D.C., for the National Capital Housing Authority (Project)

Willow Run War Town Development Project, Detroit, Mich. (Project)

New Buildings for 194X: Hotel (Project)

1944   Pennypack Store Building, Philadelphia, Pa., for the Federal Public Housing Authority

Pennypack Administration Building, Philadelphia, Pa., for the Federal Public Housing Authority

Alterations and additions to Health Clinic, 22nd and Locust Streets, Philadelphia, Pa. (Project)

1944–46   Philadelphia Psychiatric Hospital, Monument Avenue and Ford Road, Philadelphia, Pa. (Project)

1947   Alterations, Office Building and Cafeteria, Container Corporation of America, Manayunk, Pa. (Project)

1949   Coward Shoe Store, Philadelphia, Pa.

Later Work

1945–49   Residence for Dr. and Mrs. Philip Q. Roche, Harts Lane, Miquon, Whitemarsh Township, Montgomery County, Pa.

1946–54   Triangle Area Report for Philadelphia City Planning Commission, as consultant

Mill Creek Redevelopment Area Plan, Philadelphia, Pa., submitted as consultant to Philadelphia City Planning Commission (in association with Kenneth Day, Louis E. McAllister and Anne G. Tyng)

1947–49   Residence for Dr. and Mrs. Winslow T. Tompkins, proposed Apalogen Road on School House Lane, Germantown, Pa. (Project)

1948   Jefferson National Expansion Memorial, St. Louis, Mo. (Competition entry)

Interior alterations to Radbill Oil Company, 1724 Chestnut Street, Philadelphia, Pa.

1948–49   Residence for Mr. and Mrs. Morton Weiss, Whitehall Road, East Norriton Township, Montgomery County, Pa.

1949   Residence for Mr. and Mrs. Samuel Genel, NW corner Lancaster Avenue and Indian Creek Drive, Lower Merion Township, Montgomery County, Pa.

1949–50   Addition of Occupational Therapy Building to Philadelphia Psychiatric Hospital, Ford and Monument Roads, Philadelphia, Pa. (Bernard S. Pincus Building, Isadore Rosenfield, Hospital Consultant)

1950   Alterations on Saint Luke's Hospital, Philadelphia, Pa.

Residence for Mr. and Mrs. Jacob Sherman, 414 Sycamore Avenue, Lower Merion Township, Montgomery County, Pa.

1950–53   Samuel Radbill Building, Philadelphia Psychiatric Hospital (Designed in 1950)

1951   East Poplar Redevelopment Area Plan, Philadelphia, Pa. (in association with Day, McAllister and Tyng)

1951–53   Southwest Temple Redevelopment Area Plan, Philadelphia, Pa. (in association with Day, McAllister and Tyng)

Yale University Art Gallery, New Haven, Conn. (in association with Douglas I. Orr)

1952–53   Mill Creek Public Housing Project I, 46 Street and Fairmount Avenue, Philadelphia, Pa. (Kenneth Day and Louis E. McAllister, Associated)

1953   Residence for Mr. and Mrs. Ralph Roberts, School House Lane, Germantown, Pa. (Project)

1954   Adath Jeshurun Synagogue, Elkins Park, Pa. (Project)

Residence for Dr. and Mrs. Francis Adler, Davidson Road, Philadelphia, Pa. (Project)

Residence for Mr. Weber DeVore, Montgomery Avenue, Springfield Township, Montgomery County, Pa. (Project)

48 1954–56 American Federation of Labor Medical Service Plan Building, Philadelphia, Pa.

1954–59 Trenton Jewish Community Center, Trenton, N.J. (Project)

1955 Residence Alteration, house of Dr. and Mrs. Francis Adler, Germantown, Pa. (Kitchen alteration)

1955–56 Bath House, Trenton Jewish Community Center, Trenton, N.J. Day Camp 1956–57

1955–57 R.I.A.S., Research Institution for Advanced Study, Glenn L. Martin Company, Fort Meade, Md. (Project)

1956 Library, Washington University, St. Louis, Mo. (Competition entry)

1956–57 Planning Studies of Penn Center and Midtown Traffic for Philadelphia, Pa. (Project)

Enrico Fermi Memorial Competition, Chicago, Ill. (Competition entry)

1957 A City Tower ("Tomorrow's City Hall") (Project) Concrete Institute (Anne Griswold Tyng associate)

1957–59 Alterations and additions to the residence of Irving L. and Dorothy E. Shaw, 2129 Cypress Street, Philadelphia, Pa.

1957–61 Alfred Newton Richards Medical Research Building, 3700 Hamilton Walk, University of Pennsylvania, Philadelphia, Pa.

Residence of Mr. and Mrs. Fred E. Clever, Hunt Tract, Delaware Township, Camden County, N.J.

1957—— Biology Building, 2800 Hamilton Walk, University of Pennsylvania, Philadelphia, Pa. (Under construction 1961—)

1958 Residence for Mr. Lawrence Morris, Mount Kisco, N.Y. (Project)

1958–61 Tribune Review Publishing Company Building, Greensburg, Pa.

1959 Residence for Mr. Robert H. Fleisher, Woodland Glen, Elkins Park, Pa. (Project)

Residence for Mr. and Mrs. M. Morton Goldenberg, Hemlock Hedges, Frazer Road, Rydal, Pa. (Project)

1959—— First Unitarian Church, Rochester, N.Y. (Under construction, 1962)

Salk Institute for Biological Studies, San Diego, Cal. (Working drawings are in preparation, 1962)

1959–61 Residence of Dr. and Mrs. Bernard Shapiro, Hidden River Road, Penn Valley, Narberth, Pa.

U.S. Consulate Buildings for Angola, Luanda, Portuguese Angola. Chancellery and residence (Project in abeyance)

Residence for a Single Person, Chestnut Hill, Pa.

1959–62 Mill Creek Public Housing Project II, Row Housing and Community Center, 46th and Aspen Streets, Philadelphia, Pa.

1960 Residence for Dr. and Mrs. Norman Fisher, Hatboro, Pa. (Under design)

1960—— Bristol Township Municipal Building, Bristol, Levittown, Pa. (Under design)

Dormitories, Bryn Mawr College, Bryn Mawr, Pa. (Under design)

1960–61 Franklin Delano Roosevelt Memorial Competition, Washington, D.C. (Competition entry)

1961 Barge on the Thames, England, for American Wind Symphony, Pittsburgh, Pa.

Carborundum Company, Niagara Falls, N.Y., Warehouse and Regional Sales Office, Atlanta, Ga., and Mountainview, Cal. (Project)

Plymouth Swim Club, Plymouth Township, Pa. (Project)

General Motors Exhibition, 1964 World's Fair, New York, N.Y. (Project)

1961–62 Market City East Redevelopment Project. Study made for City of Philadelphia and Graham Foundation (Under design)

1961—— Chemistry Building, University of Virginia, Charlottesville, Va. (Under design)

Fine Arts Building for Fort Wayne Fine Arts Foundation, Inc., 232½ West Wayne Street, Fort Wayne, Ind. (Under design)

Shapero Hall of Pharmacy, Wayne State University, Detroit, Mich. (Project)

Mikveh Israel Synagogue, Philadelphia, Pa. (Under design)

United Neighborhood Playground, Riverside Drive, New York, N.Y., with Isamu Noguchi (Under design)

1. *Siena. Sketch by Louis I. Kahn, 1928–29.*

2. *Alfred Newton Richards Medical Research Building, University of Pennsylvania. Perspective drawing, 1960.*
    (Photo courtesy of the Museum of Modern Art, New York)

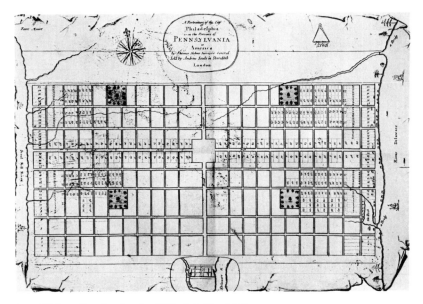

3. *William Penn's plan for Philadelphia, 1683.*

4. *Frank Furness. Guarantee Safe Deposit and Trust Company (Tradesmen's National Bank and Trust Company), Philadelphia, 1875. Now demolished.*

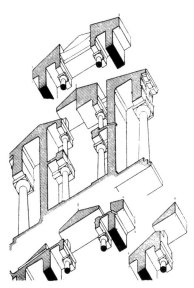

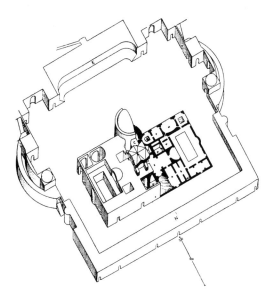

5. *Auguste Choisy. Axonometric section of a Greek temple.*

6. *Auguste Choisy. Axonometric drawing of the Baths of Caracalla.*

7. *A Shopping Center. Plan and elevations, student drawing, 1924.*

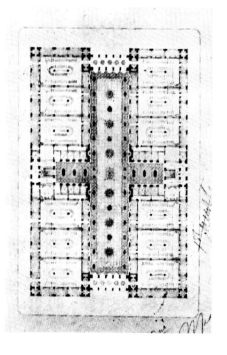

8. *John Molitor, supervisory architect. Main Portico, Palace of Liberal Arts, Sesquicentennial International Exposition, Philadelphia, 1926. Rendering by Louis I. Kahn.*

9. *San Gimignano. Sketch, 1928–29.*

10. *Paul P. Cret. Folger Shakespeare Library, Washington, D.C., 1929–32.*

11. *Howe and Lescaze. Philadelphia Saving Fund Society Building, Philadelphia, 1930–32. While under construction. (Photo courtesy of the Museum of Modern Art, New York)*

12. *Synagogue Ahavath Israel, North Philadelphia, 1935–37.*

13A. *Slum Block Rebuilding Project, 1933. Alfred Kastner, principal architect; Louis I. Kahn, assistant architect and co-designer, Jersey Homesteads Cooperative Development, Hightstown, New Jersey, 1935–37. Unit under construction.*

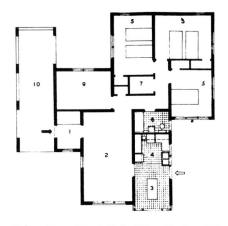

13B. *Slum Block Rebuilding Project. Plan.*

13C. *Slum Block Rebuilding Project. Model.*

14. *Howe, Stonorov, and Kahn. Carver Court Housing Development, Coatesville, Pennsylvania, 1941–43.*

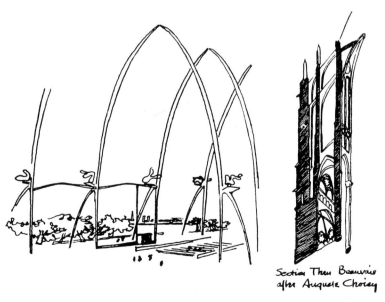

Section Thru Beauvais
after Auguste Choisy

15. *Sketch for monument and section through Beauvais Cathedral, after Choisy.*

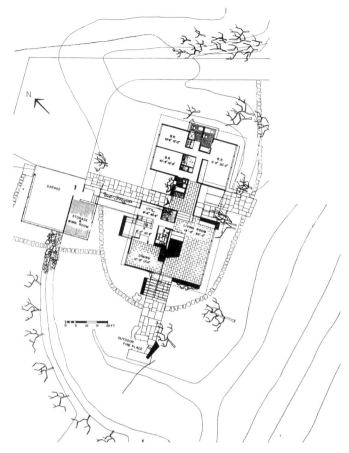

16.   *Weiss House, Norristown, Pennsylvania, 1948–49. Plan.*

17A.   *Weiss House. South side with double-hung window and panel wall.*

17B.   *Weiss House. Fireplace.*

18. *Samuel Genel House, Lower Merion Township, Pennsylvania, Garden court, 1949.*

19. *Bernard S. Pincus Occupational Therapy Building, Philadelphia Psychiatric Hospital, 1949–50. Interior.*

20. *Samuel Radbill Building, Philadelphia Psychiatric Hospital, 1950–53.*

21. *Hypostyle Hall, Karnak. Drawing, 1951.*

22. *Acropolis, Athens. Drawing, 1951.*

23. *Delphi from Marmaria. Drawing, 1951.*

24.   *Temple of Hera II, Paestum. Detail.*

25.   *"Teatro Marittimo," Hadrian's Villa, Tivoli.*

26. *Ludwig Mies van der Rohe.*
    Alumni Memorial Hall, Illinois
    Institute of Technology, Chicago, 1945–46.

27. *Alvar Aalto. Baker House*
    Dormitory, Massachusetts Institute of
    Technology, Cambridge, Massachusetts, 1947–48.

29. *Le Corbusier. Maisons Jaoul, Neuilly, 1952.*

28. *Le Corbusier. Unité d'Habitation,*
    Marseilles, 1946–48.

30A.   *Louis I. Kahn in association with Douglas Orr. Yale University Art Gallery,*
New Haven, Connecticut, 1951–53. View from Weir Courtyard at night.

30B.   *Yale University Art Gallery. View from Weir Courtyard (north façade).*

31.   *Yale University Art Gallery. Perspective study of entrance
and south façade, showing proposed vaults, 1952.*

32. *Yale University Art Gallery. View from west.*

33. *Yale University Art Gallery.*
    Reflected ceiling plan.

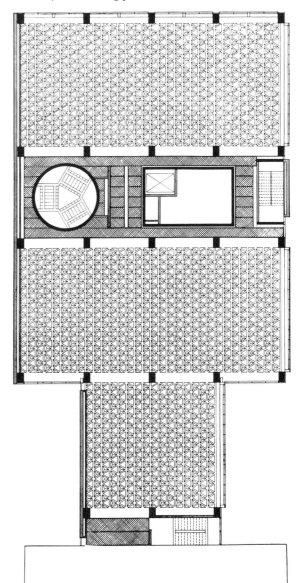

34. *R. Buckminster Fuller and one of his cardboard domes, Yale University, 1953.*

35. *Yale University Art Gallery. Main floor looking west.*

36. *Yale University Art Gallery. Interior of stair tower.*

37.   *Yale University Art Gallery. Interior with pogo panels, looking east.*

38.   *Yale University Art Gallery. Third floor, looking east.*

39. *Louis I. Kahn in association with Kenneth Day and Louis McAllister. Mill Creek Public Housing Project I, Philadelphia, 1952–53.*

40. *Adath Jeshurun Synagogue, Elkins Park, Pennsylvania, project, 1954. Plan.*

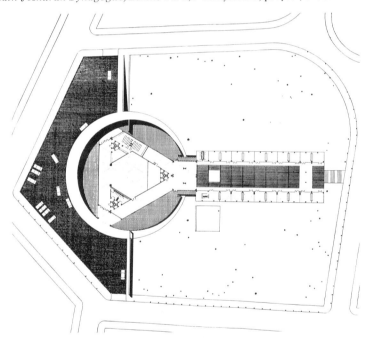

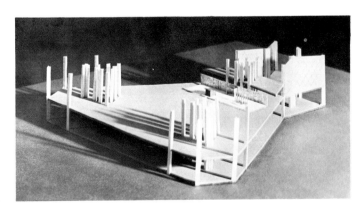

41. *Adath Jeshurun Synagogue. Model.*

42.   *Adler House, project, 1955. Elevation.*

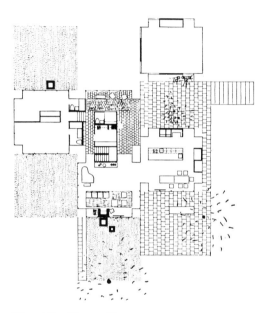

43.   *Adler House. Plan.*

44.   *De Vore House, project, 1955. Plan.*

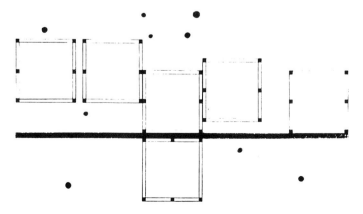

45.   *A.F. of L. Medical Service Plan Building, Philadelphia, 1954–56. Interior.*

46.   *A.F. of L. Medical Service Plan Building. Exterior.*

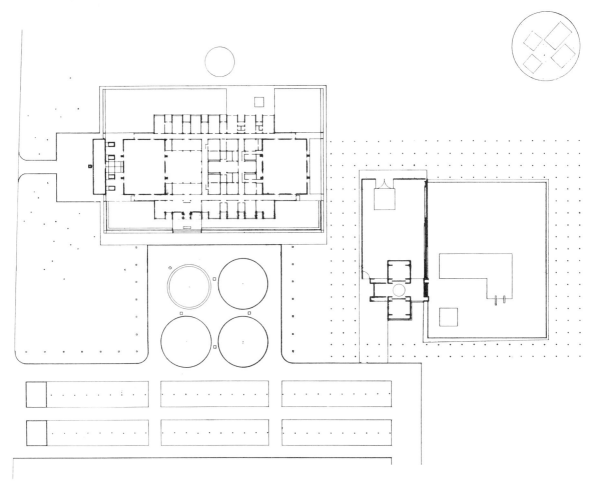

47. *Trenton Jewish Community Center, Trenton, New Jersey, 1954–59. Plot plan. Center: Main building, final version of p.*
Right: Bath House and pool, 1955–56. Upper right: Day camp, 1956–57.

48. *Bath House, Trenton Jewish Community Center, 1955–56. Plan and roof plan.*

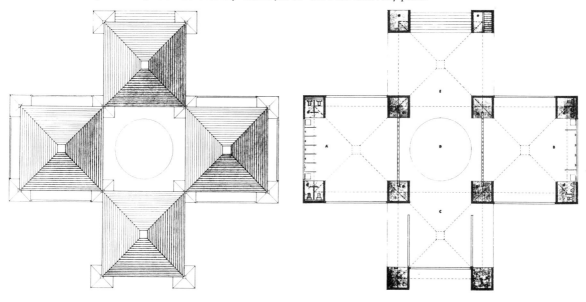

49. *Trenton Bath House. Central court.*

t.

50. *Trenton Bath House. Changing room.*

51. *Trenton Bath House. Exterior detail.*

52. *Frank Lloyd Wright. Hillside Home School,*
    Spring Green, Wisconsin, 1902.

53. *Main building, Trenton Jewish Community Center, project. Plan.*

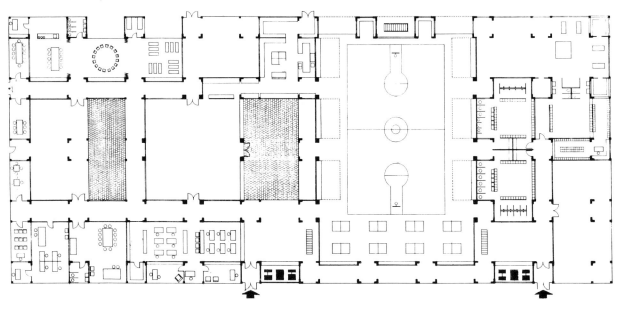

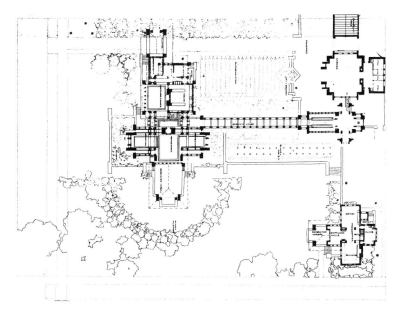

54.   *Frank Lloyd Wright. Martin House, Buffalo, New York, 1904. Plan.*

55.   *Main building, Trenton Jewish Community Center. Ceiling plan.*

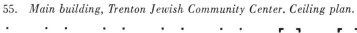

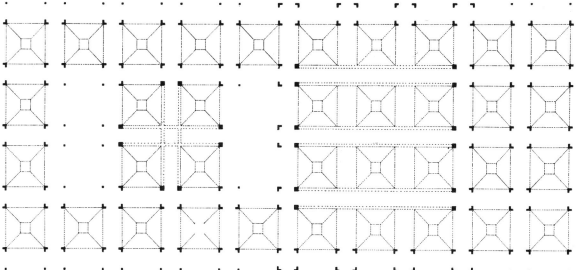

56.   *Main building, Trenton Jewish Community Center. Model.*

57. *Library, Washington University, St. Louis, Missouri, competition entry, 1956. Reflected ceiling plan.*

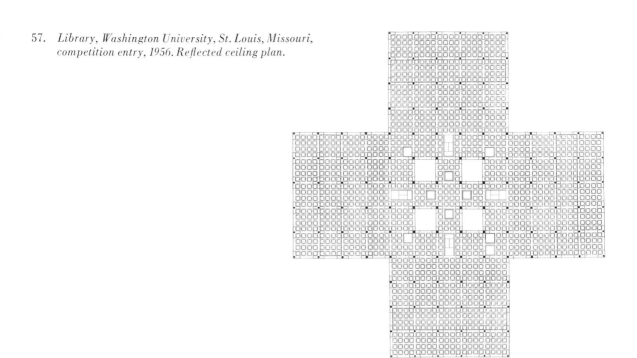

58. *Library, Washington University, competition entry. Perspective and elevation.*

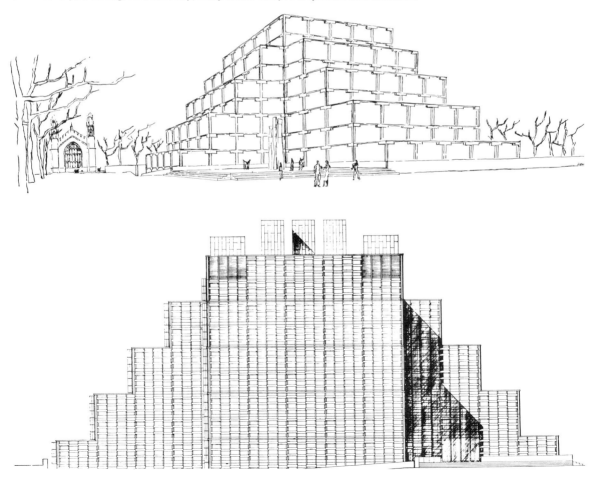

59. *Research Institution for Advanced Study for Glenn L. Martin Company, Fort Meade, Maryland, project, 1955–57. Model.*

60. *City Hall, Philadelphia, project, 1952–53. Model and perspective drawing.*

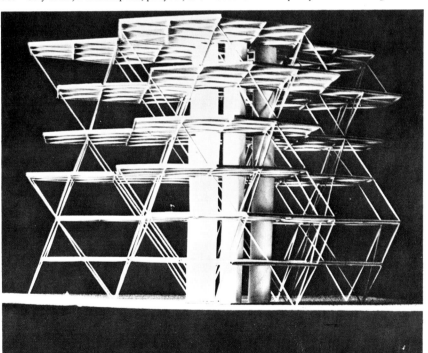

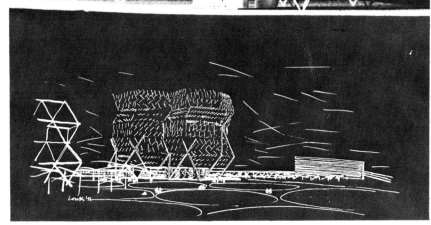

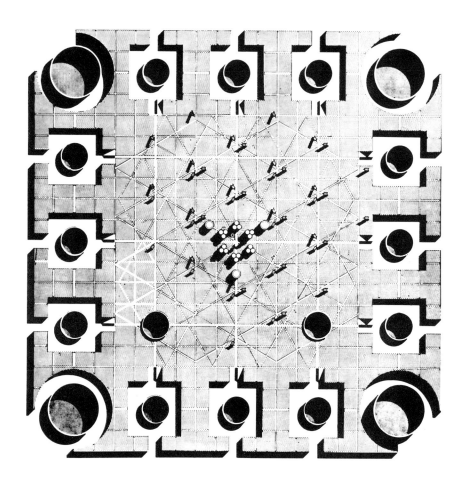

61. *A city tower, "Tomorrow's City Hall," study for the*
    Universal Atlas Cement Company, 1957. Model of parking plaza.

62. *A city tower. Model of tower and plaza, detail.*

A

63. *A city tower. A. Elevation of model as glazed. B. Section. C. Typical floor plan.*

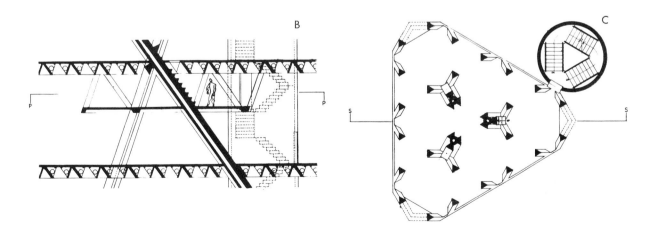

B

C

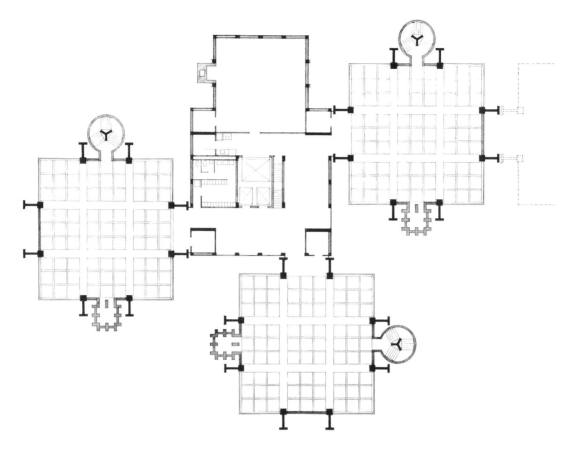

64. *Alfred Newton Richards Medical Research Building, University of Pennsylvania,*
Philadelphia, 1957–61. Early plan.

65. *Richards Medical Research Building.*
Perspective study, intermediate version.
(Photo courtesy of the Museum of Modern Art, New York)

66. *Richards Medical Research Building and Biology Building. A. North elevation.*
B. First-floor plan. C. Fifth-floor plan.

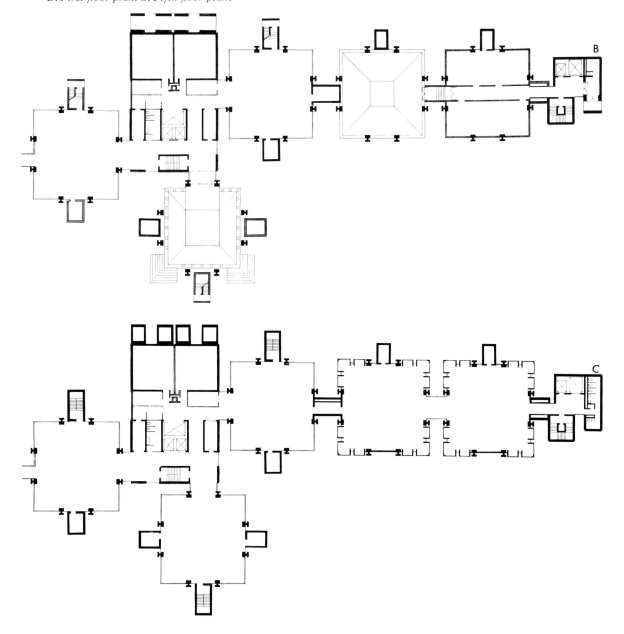

67. *Richards Medical Research Building. During construction.*

68. *Richards Medical Research Building. Entrance.*

69. *Richards Medical Research Building. Entrance portico under main laboratory tower.*

70. *Richards Medical Research Building. Laboratory towers and service stacks from the north.*

71. *Richards Medical Research Building. Exterior stair towers (right and left)
and four air-intake stacks from the south.*

72. *Richards Medical Research Building. View from corridor, showing adjacent laboratory towers.*

73. *Richards Medical Research Building. Interior of typical laboratory studio before partitioning.*

74. *Richards Medical Research Building and Biology Building. Model, showing north and west elevations. (Photo courtesy of the Museum of Modern Art, New York).*

75. *Frank Lloyd Wright, Larkin Building, Buffalo, New York, 1903—04. Interior (building now demolished).*

76. *Larkin Building. Drawing. (Both Larkin Building photos courtesy of the Museum of Modern Art, New York).*

77. *Morris House, Mt. Kisco, New York, project, 1958.*

78.   *Tribune Review Publishing Company Building,*
       Greensburg, Pennsylvania, 1958–61. North side.

79.   *Tribune Review Building. East front.*

80. *Tribune Review Building. East front, detail.*

81. *Tribune Review Building. Business office.*

82. *Mill Creek Public Housing Project II, Philadelphia,*
1959–62. Row housing under construction.

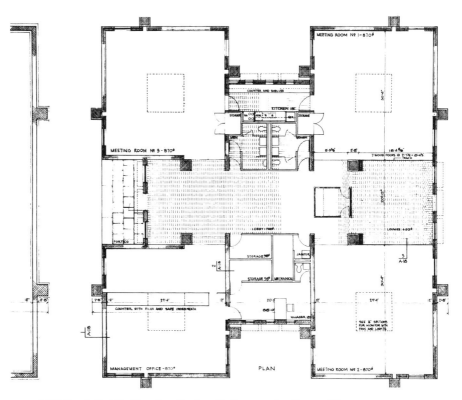

83. *Mill Creek Public Housing Project II. Community Center. Plan.*

84A. *Mill Creek Public Housing Project II. Community Center.*
       Exterior during construction.

84B. *Mill Creek Public Housing Project II. View from southeast during construction.*

85. *Mill Creek Public Housing Project II. Community Center. Interior, during construction.*

84C. *Mill Creek Public Housing Project II. View from east during construction.*

86. *Frank Lloyd Wright. Unity Church, Oak Park, Illinois, 1906.*

87. *Unity Church. Plan.*

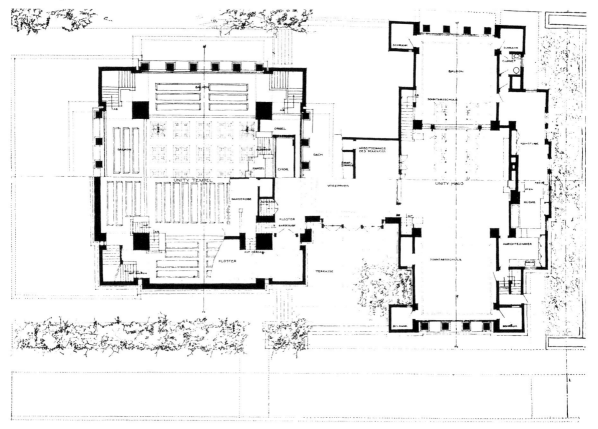

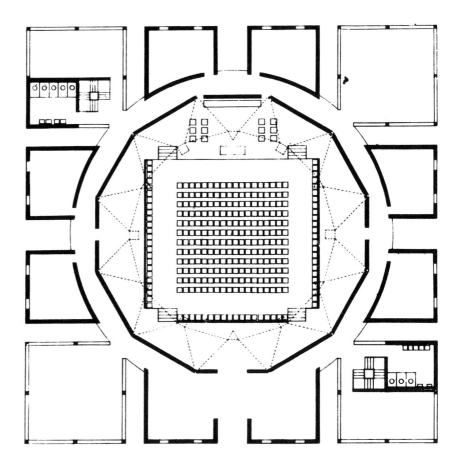

88. *First Unitarian Church, Rochester, New York,*
     1959–. Plan and models, first stage.

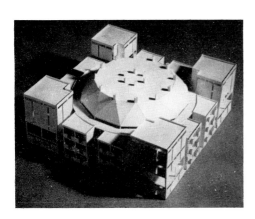

89. *First Unitarian Church. Plan and elevations, final stage. 1. Meeting room 2. Lobby 3. Library 4. Inglenook 5. Women's workroom 6. Committee room 7. Minister's room.*

Stage 5

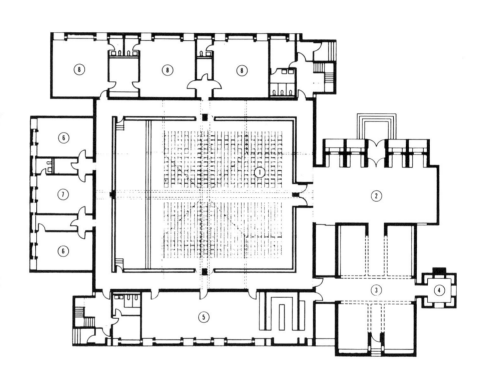

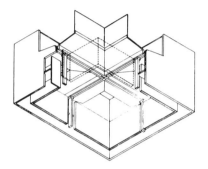

90. *First Unitarian Church.*
     Isometric drawing.

91. *First Unitarian Church.*
     Longitudinal section.

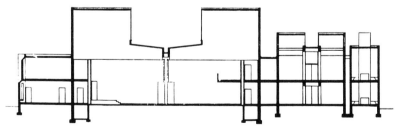

92. *Goldenberg House. View of model from above.*

93. *Goldenberg House, Rydal, Pennsylvania, project, 1959. Plan.*

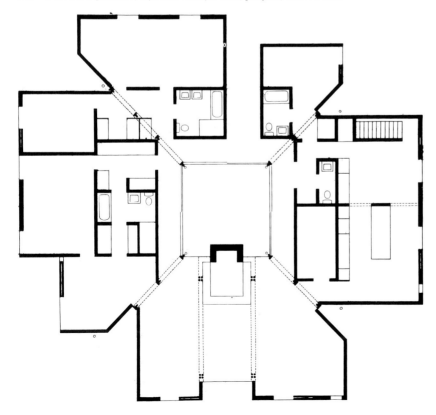

94. *Goldenberg House. Early model, side elevation.*

95. *House for a single person, Chestnut Hill,*
     Pennsylvania, 1959–61. Entrance side.

96. *House for a single person,*
     Chestnut Hill. Kitchen side.

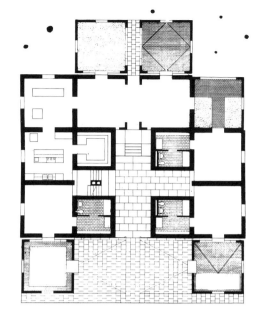

97.   *Fleisher House, Elkins Park, Pennsylvania, project, 1959. Plan.*

98A.   *Fleisher House. Model. Entrance side.*

98B.   *Fleisher House. Model. Garden side.*

99. *U.S. Consulate, Luanda, Portuguese Angola, project, 1959–62. Plot plan.*

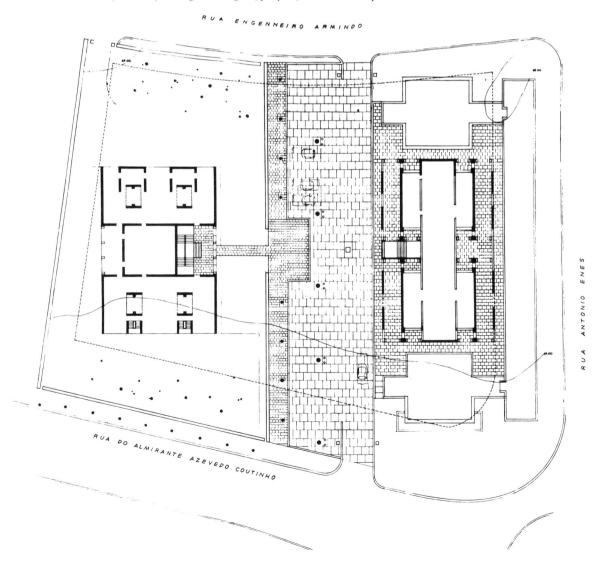

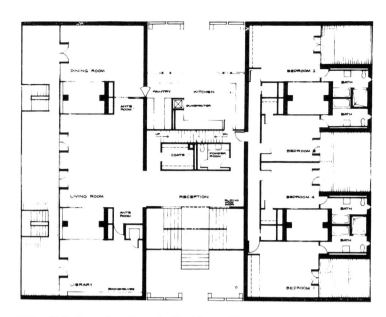

100.   *U.S. Consulate, Luanda. Residence. Plan.*

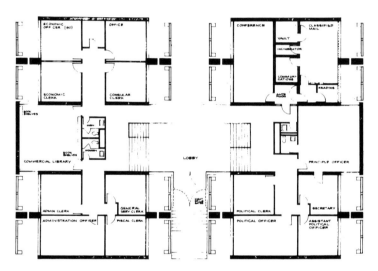

101.   *U.S. Consulate, Luanda. Chancellery. Plan.*

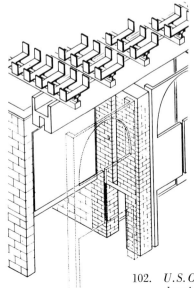

102.   *U.S. Consulate, Luanda. Chancellery. Isometric
drawing of wall and sun control systems.*

103. *U.S. Consulate, Luanda. Model.*

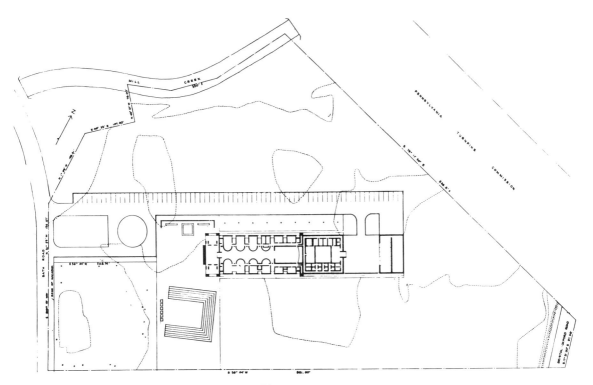

104. *Town Hall, Bristol, Pennsylvania, 1960 — . Plan.*

105. *Jonas Salk Institute for Biological Studies, San Diego, California, 1959 — . Site model from above.*

106. *Salk Institute. Site model from the west.*

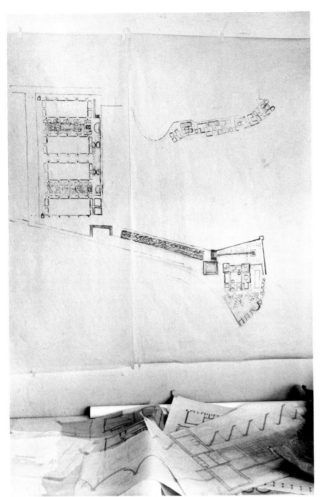

107. *Salk Institute. Sketch plan.*

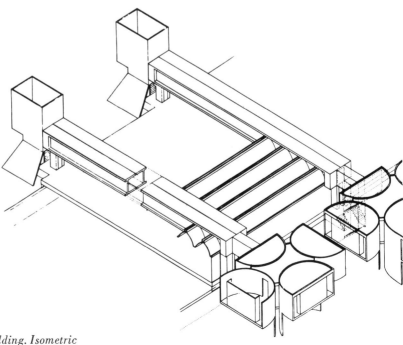

108. *Salk Institute. Research Building. Isometric
drawing of laboratories and studies at early stage.*

109. *Salk Institute. Research Building. Section of model.*

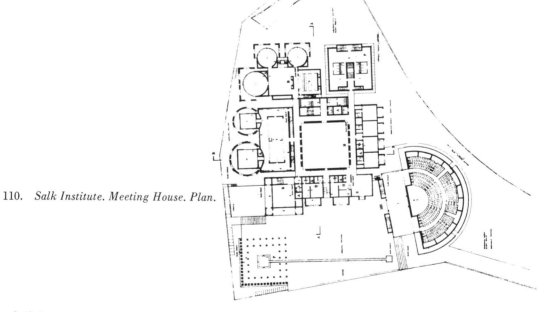

110. *Salk Institute. Meeting House. Plan.*

111. *Salk Institute. Research Building. Longitudinal section of two units.*

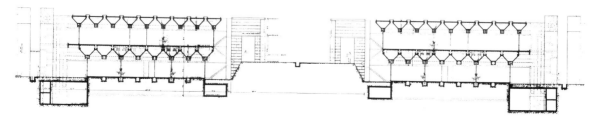

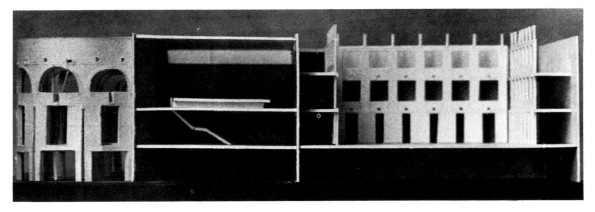

112.   *Salk Institute. Meeting House. Model, showing section of court.*

113.   *Salk Institute. Meeting House. Model. West elevation.*

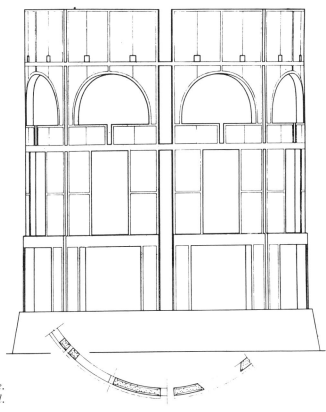

114.   *Salk Institute. Meeting House.*
       Screen wall. Elevation detail.

115. *Composite plan of Rome, from plans by Giovanni Battista Piranesi, 1762 (?).*

116. *Comlongan Castle, Dumphriesshire. Plan.*

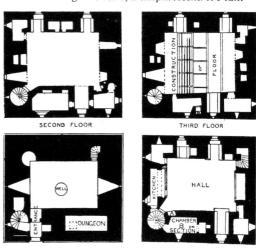

117. *Dormitory, Bryn Mawr College, Bryn Mawr, Pennsylvania, 1960 —. Second-floor plan.*

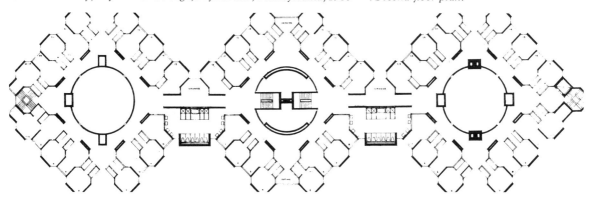

118.   *American Wind Symphony Barge
on the Thames, London, England, 1961.*

119.   *General Motors Exhibition, 1964 World's Fair, New York City, project, 1961. Study sketch.*

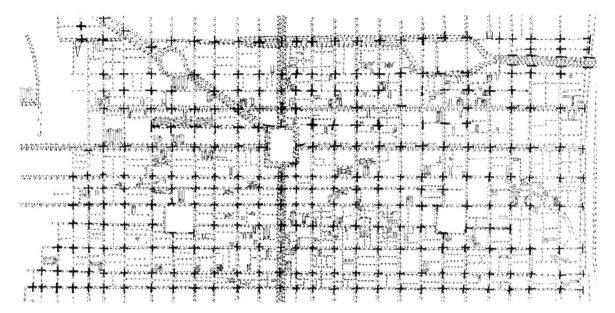

120A. *Philadelphia. Existing movement pattern.*

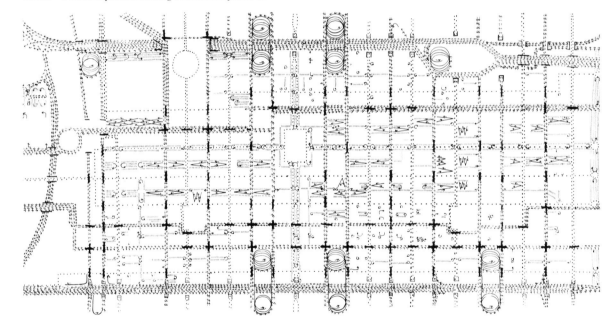

120B. *Philadelphia. Proposed movement pattern, 1952–53.*

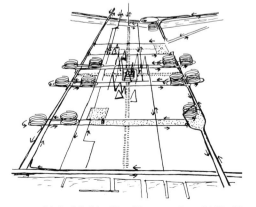

121. *Philadelphia City Plan, project, 1952–53.*

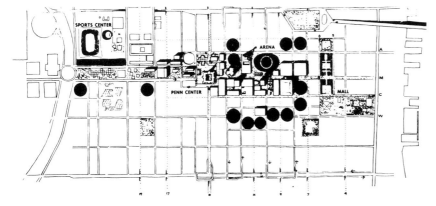

122.   *Philadelphia City Plan, project, 1956–57. Plan.*

123.   *Proposal for Center City, Philadelphia, project, 1956 — . Perspective drawing.*

124.   *Parking Garage and Shopping Tower for Philadelphia,*
       project, 1956–57. Section and perspective drawing.

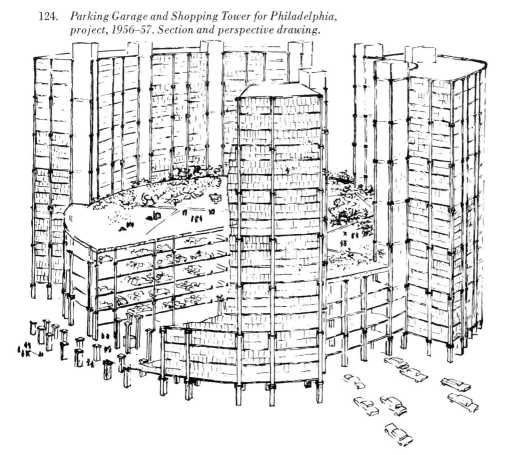

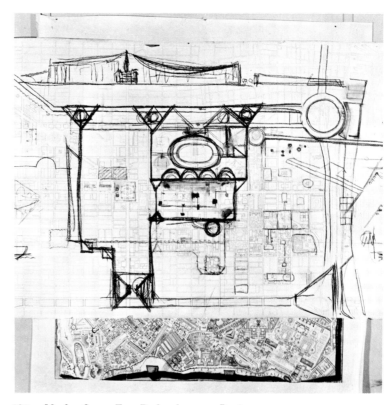

125. *Market Street East Redevelopment Project,*
Philadelphia, 1961 — . Plan.

126. *Market Street East. Model.*

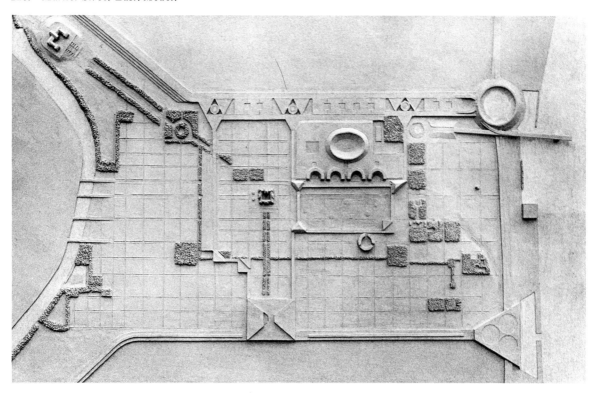

127. *Carcassonne, drawing by Viollet-le-Duc, 1878.*

128. *Market Street East. Traffic pattern.*

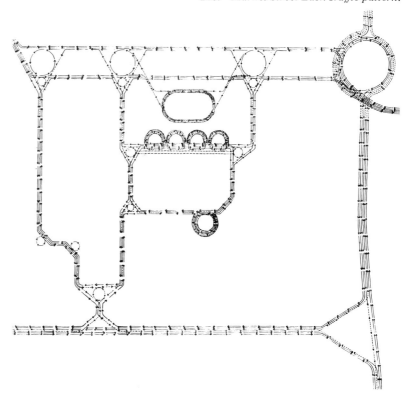

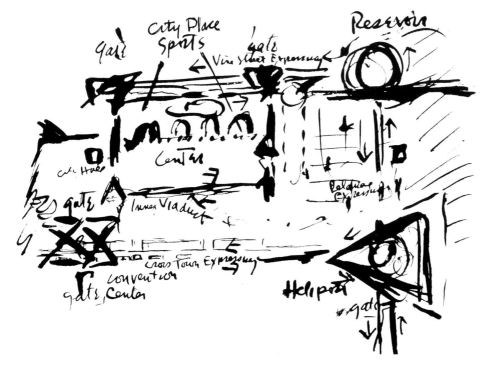

129. *Market Street East. Sketch plan.*

130. *Market Street East. Sections.*

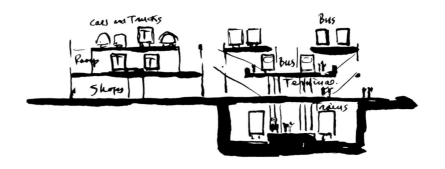

Two Statements by Louis Kahn

Order is
Design is form-making in order
Form emerges out of a system of construction
Growth is a construction
In order is creative force
In design is the means—where   with what   when   with how much
The nature of space reflects what it wants to be
    Is the auditorium a Stradivarius
      or is it an ear
    Is the auditorium a creative instrument
      keyed to Bach or Bartok
      played by the conductor
      or is it a convention hall
In the nature of space is the spirit and the will to exist a certain way
    Design must closely follow that will
    Therefore a stripe painted horse is not a zebra.
    Before a railroad station is a building
    it wants to be a street
    it grows out of the needs of street
      out of the order of movement
    A meeting of contours englazed.
Thru the nature—why
Thru the order—what
Thru design—how
A Form emerges from the structural elements inherent in the form.
A dome is not conceived when questions arise how to build it.
    Nervi grows an arch
    Fuller grows a dome
Mozart's compositions are designs
    They are exercises of order—intuitive
    Design encourages more designs
    Designs derive their imagery from order
    Imagery is the memory—the Form
    Style is an adopted order
The same order created the elephant and created man
    They are different designs
    Begun from different aspirations
    Shaped from different circumstances
Order does not imply Beauty
    The same order created the dwarf and Adonis
Design is not making Beauty
    Beauty emerges from selection
      affinities
      integration
      love
Art is a form making life in order—psychic
Order is intangible
    It is a level of creative consciousness
    forever becoming higher in level
    The higher the order the more diversity in design

Order supports integration
From what the space wants to be the unfamiliar may be revealed
to the architect.
From order he will derive creative force and power of self-
criticism
to give form to this unfamiliar.
Beauty will evolve

(*From Perspecta, 3, 1955, with the permission of the author and the editors.*)

Form and Design

A young architect came to ask a question. 'I dream of spaces full of wonder. Spaces that rise and envelop flowingly without beginning, without end, of a jointless material white and gold.' 'When I place the first line on paper to capture the dream, the dream becomes less.'

This is a good question. I once learned that a good question is greater than the most brilliant answer.

This is a question of the unmeasurable and the measurable. Nature, physical nature, is measurable.

Feeling and dream has no measure, has no language, and everyone's dream is singular.

Everything that is made however obeys the laws of nature. The man is always greater than his works because he can never fully express his aspirations. For to express oneself in music or architecture is by the measurable means of composition or design. The first line on paper is already a measure of what cannot be expressed fully. The first line on paper is less.

'Then,' said the young architect, 'what should be the discipline, what should be the ritual that brings one closer to the psyche. For in this aura of no material and no language, I feel man truly is.'

Turn to Feeling and away from Thought. In Feeling is the Psyche. Thought is Feeling and presence of Order. Order, the maker of all existence, has No Existence Will. I choose the word Order instead of knowledge because personal knowledge is too little to express Thought abstractly. This Will is in the Psyche.

All that we desire to create has its beginning in feeling alone. This is true for the scientist. It is true for the artist. But I warned that to remain in Feeling away from Thought means to make nothing.

Said the young architect: 'To live and make nothing is intolerable. The dream has in it already the *will to be* and the desire to express this *will*. Thought is inseparable from Feeling. In what way then can Thought enter creation so that this psychic will can be more closely expressed? This is my next question.'

When personal feeling transcends into Religion (not a religion but the essence religion) and Thought leads to Philosophy, the mind opens to realizations. Realization of what may be the *existence will* of, let us say, particular architectural spaces. Realization is the merg-

ing of Thought and Feeling at the closest rapport of the mind with
the Psyche, the source of *what a thing wants to be.*

It is the beginning of Form. Form encompasses a harmony of systems, a sense of Order and that which characterizes one existence from another. Form has no shape or dimension. For example, in the differentiation of a spoon from spoon, spoon characterizes a form having two inseparable parts, the handle and the bowl. A spoon implies a specific design made of silver or wood, big or little, shallow or deep. Form is 'what.' Design is 'how.' Form is impersonal. Design belongs to the designer. Design is a circumstantial act, how much money there is available, the site, the client, the extent of knowledge. Form has nothing to do with circumstantial conditions. In architecture, it characterizes a harmony of spaces good for a certain activity of man.

Reflect then on what characterizes abstractly House, a house, home. House is the abstract characteristic of spaces good to live in. House is the form, in the mind of wonder it should be there without shape or dimension. *A* house is a conditional interpretation of these spaces. This is design. In my opinion the greatness of the architect depends on his powers of realization of that which is House, rather than his design of *a* house which is a circumstantial act. Home is the house and the occupants. Home becomes different with each occupant.

The client for whom a house is designed states the areas he needs. The architect creates spaces out of those required areas. It may also be said that this house created for the particular family must have the character of being good for another. The design in this way reflects its trueness to Form.

I think of school as an environment of spaces where it is good to learn. Schools began with a man under a tree who did not know he was a teacher discussing his realization with a few who did not know they were students. The students reflected on what was exchanged and how good it was to be in the presence of this man. They aspired that their sons also listen to such a man. Soon spaces were erected and the first schools became. The establishment of school was inevitable because it was part of the desires of man. Our vast systems of education, now vested in Institutions, stem from these little schools but the spirit of their beginning is now forgotten. The rooms required by our institutions of learning are stereotype and uninspiring. The Institute's required uniform classrooms, the locker-lined corridors and other so-called functional areas and devices, are certainly arranged in neat packages by the architect who follows closely the areas and budgetary limits as required by the school authorities. The schools are good to look at but are shallow in architecture because they do not reflect the spirit of the man under the tree. The entire system of schools that followed from the beginning would not have been possible if the beginning were not in harmony with the nature of man. It can also be said that the existence will of school was there even before the circumstances of the man under a tree.

That is why it is good for the mind to go back to the beginning because the beginning of any established activity of man is its most wonderful moment. For in it lies all its spirit and resourcefulness, from which we must constantly draw our inspirations of present needs. We can make our institutions great by giving them our sense of this inspiration in the architecture we offer them.

Reflect then on the meaning of school, *a* school, institution. The institution is the authority from whom we get their requirements of areas. A School or a specific design is what the institution expects of us. But School, the spirit school, the essence of the existence will, is what the architect should convey in his design. And I say he must, even if the design does not correspond to the budget. Thus the architect is distinguished from the mere designer. In school as a realm of spaces where it is good to learn, the lobby measured by the institute as so many square feet per student would become a generous Pantheon-like space where it is good to enter. The corridors would be transferred into classrooms belonging to the students themselves by making them much wider and provided with alcoves overlooking the gardens. They would become the places where boy meets girl, where the student discusses the work of the professor with his fellow-student. By allowing classroom time to these spaces instead of passage time from class to class, it would become a meeting connection and not merely a corridor, which means a place of possibilities in self-learning. It becomes the classroom belonging to the students. The classrooms should evoke their use by their space variety and not follow the usual soldier-like dimensional similarity, because one of the most wonderful spirits of this man under the tree is his recognition of the singularity of every man. A teacher or a student is not the same when he is with a few in an intimate room with a fireplace as in a large high room with many others. And must the cafeteria be in the basement, even though its use in time is little? Is not the relaxing moment of the meal also a part of learning?

As I write alone in my office, I feel differently about the very same things that I talked about only a few days ago to many at Yale. Space has power and gives mode.

This, with the singularity of every person, suggests a variety of spaces with a variety of the ways of natural light and orientation to compass and garden. Such spaces lend themselves to ideas in the curriculum, to better connection between teacher and student, and to vitality in the development of the institution.

The realization of what particularizes the domain of spaces good for school would lead an institution of learning to challenge the architect to awareness of what School *wants to be* which is the same as saying what is the form, School.

In the same spirit I should like to talk about a Unitarian Church.

The very first day I talked before the congregation using a blackboard. From what I heard the minister speak about with men around I realized that the form aspect, the form realization of Unitarian activity was bound around that which is Question. Question eternal of why anything. I had to come to the realization of what existence will and what order of spaces were expressive of the Question.

I drew a diagram on the blackboard which I believe served as the Form drawing of the church and, of course, was not meant to be a suggested design.

I made a square center in which I placed a question mark. Let us say I meant it to be the sanctuary. This I encircled with an ambulatory for those who did not want to go into the sanctuary. Around the ambulatory I drew a corridor which belonged to an outer circle enclosing a space, *the school*. It was clear that School which gives rise to Question became the wall which surrounds Question. This was the form expression of the church, not the design.

This puts me in mind of the meaning of Chapel in a university.

Is it the mosaics, stained glass, water effects and other known devices? Is it not the place of inspired ritual which could be expressed by a student who winked at chapel as he passed it after being given a sense of dedication to this work by a great teacher. He did not need to go in.

It may be expressed by a place which for the moment is left undescribed and has an ambulatory for the one who does not want to enter it. The ambulatory is surrounded by an arcade for the one who prefers not to go into the ambulatory. The arcade sits in the garden for the one who prefers not to enter the arcade. The garden has a wall and the student can be outside winking at it. The ritual is inspired and not set and is the basis of the form Chapel.

Back to the Unitarian Church. My first design solution which followed was a completely symmetrical square. The building provided for the schoolrooms around the periphery, the corners were punctuated by larger rooms. The space in the centre of the square harboured the sanctuary and the ambulatory. This design closely resembled the diagram on the blackboard and everyone liked it until the particular interests of every committee member began to eat away at the rigid geometry. But the original premise still held of the school around the sanctuary.

It is the role of design to adjust to the circumstantial. At one stage of discussion with the members of the church committee a few insisted that the sanctuary be separated entirely from the school. I said fine, let's put it that way and I then put the auditorium in one place and connected it up with a very neat little connector to the school. Soon everyone realized that the coffee hour after the ceremony brought several related rooms next to the sanctuary, which when alone were too awkwardly self-satisfying and caused the duplication of these rooms in the separated school block. Also, the schoolrooms by separation lost their power to evoke their use for religious and intellectual purposes and, like a stream, they all came back around the sanctuary.

The final design does not correspond to the first design though the form held.

I want to talk about the difference between form and design, about realization, about the measurable and the unmeasurable aspects of our work and about the limits of our work.

Giotto was a great painter because he painted the skies black for the daytime and he painted birds that couldn't fly and dogs that couldn't run and he made men bigger than doorways because he was a painter. A painter has this prerogative. He doesn't have to answer to the problems of gravity, nor to the images as we know them in real life. As a painter he expresses a reaction to nature and he teaches us through his eyes and his reactions to the nature of man. A sculptor is one who modifies space with the objects expressive again of his reactions to nature. He does not create space. He modifies space. An architect creates space.

Architecture has limits.

When we touch the invisible walls of its limits then we know more about what is contained in them. A painter can paint square wheels on a cannon to express the futility of war. A sculptor can carve the same square wheels. But an architect must use round wheels. Though painting and sculpture play a beautiful role in the realm of architecture as architecture plays a beautiful role in the realms of painting and sculpture, one does not have the same discipline as the other.

One may say that architecture is the thoughtful making of spaces. It is, note, the filling of areas prescribed by the client. It is the creating of spaces that evoke a feeling of appropriate use.

To the musician a sheet of music is seeing from what he hears. A plan of a building should read like a harmony of spaces in light.

Even a space intended to be dark should have just enough light from some mysterious opening to tell us how dark it really is. Each space must be defined by its structure and the character of its natural light. Of course I am not speaking about minor areas which serve the major spaces. An architectural space must reveal the evidence of its making by the space itself. It cannot be a space when carved out of a greater structure meant for a greater space because the choice of a structure is synonymous with the light and which gives image to that space. Artificial light is a single tiny static moment in light and is the light of night and never can equal the nuances of mood created by the time of day and the wonder of the seasons.

A great building, in my opinion, must begin with the unmeasurable, must go through measurable means when it is being designed and in the end must be unmeasurable. The design, the making of things is a measurable act. In fact at that point, you are like physical nature itself because in physical nature everything is measurable, even that which is yet unmeasured, like the most distant stars which we can assume will be eventually measured.

But what is unmeasurable is the psychic spirit. The psyche is expressed by feeling and also thought and I believe will always be unmeasurable. I sense that the psychic Existence Will calls on nature to make what it wants to be. I think a rose wants to be a rose. Existence Will, *man*, becomes existence, through nature's law and evolution. The results are always less than the spirit of existence.

In the same way a building has to start in the unmeasurable aura and go through the measurable to be accomplished. It is the only way you can build, the only way you can get it into being is through the measurable. You must follow the laws but in the end when the building becomes part of living it evokes unmeasurable qualities. The design involving quantities of brick, method of construction, engineering is over and the spirit of its existence takes over.

Take the beautiful tower made of bronze that was erected in New York. It is a bronze lady, incomparable in beauty, but you know she has corsets for fifteen stories because the wind bracing is not seen. That which makes it an object against the wind which can be beautifully expressed, just like nature expresses the difference between the moss and the reed. The base of this building should be wider than

the top, and the columns which are on top dancing like fairies, and
the columns below growing like mad, don't have the same dimensions
because they are not the same thing. This story if told from realization of form would make a tower more expressive of the forces.
Even if it begins in its first attempts in design to be ugly it would
be led to beauty by the statement of form.

I am doing a building in Africa, which is very close to the equator.
The glare is killing, everybody looks black against the sunlight.
Light is a needed thing, but still an enemy. The relentless sun above,
the siesta comes over you like thunder.

I saw many huts that the natives made.

There were no architects there.

I came back with multiple impressions of how clever was the man
who solved the problems of sun, rain and wind.

I came to the realization that every window should have a free wall
to face. This wall receiving the light of day would have bold opening
to the sky. The glare is modified by the lighted wall and the view is
not shut off. In this way the contrast made by separated patterns of
glare which skylight grilles close to the window make is avoided.
Another realization came from the effectiveness of the use of breeze
for insulation by the making of a loose sun roof independently supported and separated from the rain roof by a head room of 6 ft.
These designs of the window and wall and of the sun and rain roofs
would tell the man on the street the way of life in Angola.

I am designing a unique research laboratory in San Diego, California.

This is how the programme started.

The director, a famous man, heard me speak in Pittsburgh. He
came to Philadelphia to see the building I had designed for the University of Pennsylvania. We went out together on a rainy day. He
said, 'How nice, a beautiful building. I didn't know a building that
went up in the air could be nice. How many square feet do you have
in this building?' I said, 'One hundred and nine thousand square
feet.' He said, 'That's about what we need.'

That was the beginning of the programme of areas. But there was
something else he said which became the Key to the entire space
environment. Namely that Medical Research does not belong entirely to medicine or the physical sciences. It belongs to Population.
He meant that anyone with a mind in the humanities, in science, or
in art could contribute to the mental environment of research leading
to discoveries in science. Without the restriction of a dictatorial programme it became a rewarding experience to participate in the projection of an evolving programme of spaces without precedence. This
is only possible because the director is a man of unique sense of environment as an inspiring thing, and he could sense the existence
will and its realization in form which the spaces I provided had.

The simple beginning requirement of the laboratories and their
services expanded to cloistered gardens and Studies over arcades
and to spaces for meeting and relaxation interwoven with unnamed
spaces for the glory of the fuller environment.

The laboratories may be characterized as the architecture of air
cleanliness and area adjustability. The architecture of the oak table

and the rug is that of the Studies.

The Medical Research Building at the University of Pennsylvania is conceived in recognition of the realizations that science laboratories are studios and that the air to breathe should be away from the air to throw away.

The normal plan of laboratories which places the work areas off one side of a public corridor and the other side provided with the stairs, elevators, animal quarters, ducts and other services. This corridor is the vehicle of the exhaust of dangerous air and also the supply of the air you breathe, all next to each other. The only distinction between one man's spaces of work from the other is the difference of the numbers on the doors.

I designed three studio towers for the University where a man may work in his bailiwick and each studio has its own escape *stairway sub tower* and *exhaust sub tower* for isotope air, germ-infected air and noxious gas.

A central building to which the three major towers cluster takes the place of the area for services which are on the other side of the normal corridor plan. This central building has nostrils for intake of fresh air away from *exhaust sub towers* of vitiated air.

This design, an outcome of the consideration of the unique use of its spaces and how they are served, characterizes what it is for.

One day I visited the site during the erection of the pre-fabricated frame of the building. The crane's 200 ft. boom picked up 25 ton members and swung them into place like matchsticks moved by the hand. I resented the garishly painted crane, this monster which humiliated my building to be out of scale. I watched the crane go through its many movements all the time calculating how many more days this 'thing' was to dominate the site and building before a flattering photograph of the building could be made.

Now I am glad of this experience because it made me aware of the meaning of the crane in design, for it is merely the extension of the arm like a hammer. Now I began to think of members 100 tons in weight lifted by bigger cranes. The great members would be only the parts of a composite column with joints like sculpture in gold and porcelain and harbouring rooms on various levels paved in marble.

These would be the stations of the great span and the entire enclosure would be sheathed with glass held in glass mullions with strands of stainless steel interwoven like threads assisting the glass and the mullions against the forces of wind.

Now the crane was a friend and the stimulus in the realization of a new form.

The institutions of cities can be made greater by the power of their architectural spaces. The meeting house in the village green has given way to the city hall which is no more the meeting place. But I sense an existence will for the arcaded city place where the fountains play, where again boy meets girl, where the city could entertain and put up our distinguished visitors, where the many societies which uphold our democratic ideals can meet in clusters of auditoria in the city place.

The motor car has completely upset the form of the city. I feel that the time has come to make the distinction between the Viaduct architecture of the car and the architecture of man's activities. The tendencies of designers to combine the two architectures in a simple design has confused the direction of planning and technology. The Viaduct architecture enters the city from outlying areas. At this point it must become more carefully made and even at great expense more strategically placed with respect to the centre.

The Viaduct architecture includes the street which in the centre of the city wants to be a building, a building with rooms below for city piping services to avoid interruption to traffic when services need repair.

The Viaduct architecture would encompass an entirely new concept of street movement which distinguished the stop and go staccato movement of the bus from the 'go' movement of the car. The area framing expressways are like rivers. These rivers need harbours. The interim streets are like canals which need docks. The harbours are the gigantic gateways expressing the *architecture of stopping*. The terminals of the Viaduct architecture, they are garages in the core, hotels and department stores around the periphery and shopping centers on the street floor.

This strategic positioning around the city centre would present a logical image of protection against the destruction of the city by the motor car. In a sense the problem of the car and city is war, and the planning for the new growth of cities is not a complacent act, but an act of emergency.

The distinction between the two architectures, the architecture of the Viaduct and the architecture of the acts of man's activities, could bring about a logic of growth and a sound positioning of enterprise.

An architect from India gave an excellent talk at the University about the fine new work of Le Corbusier and about his own work. It impressed me, however, that these beautiful works he showed were still out of context and had no position. After his lecture I was asked to remark. Somehow I was moved to go to the blackboard where I drew in the centre of the board a towering water tower, wide on top and narrow below. Like the rays of a star, I drew aqueducts radiating from the tower. This implied the coming of the trees and fertile land and a beginning of living. The buildings not yet there which would cluster around the aqueduct would have meaningful position and character.

The city would have form.

From all I have said I do not mean to imply a system of thought and work leading to realization from Form to Design.

Designs could just as well lead to realizations in Form.

This interplay is the constant excitement of Architecture.

(*From the Voice of America* Forum Lectures, *a series on* Modern American Architecture *in 1960, originally entitled* Structure and Form. *Used with the permission of the author and the United States Information Agency.*)

Bibliography

CHRONOLOGICAL LIST OF ARTICLES,

INTERVIEWS AND STATEMENTS BY KAHN

"Pencil Drawings," *Architecture* (New York), LXIII (Jan. 1931), pp. 15–17. Drawings of a piazza, San Gimignano, and a street in Positano.

"Value and Aim in Sketching," *T-Square Club Journal*, Philadelphia, I (May 1931), pp. 4, 18–21. Illustrations include a still life and five pencil sketches, mostly of Italian scenes.

"Monumentality," in Paul Zucker, ed., *New Architecture and City Planning, A Symposium*, New York, 1944 ,pp. 577–88.

Oskar Stonorov and Louis I. Kahn, *Why City Planning is Your Responsibility*, New York, Revere Copper and Brass, Inc., 1943.

Oscar Stonorov and Louis I. Kahn, *You and Your Neighborhood . . . A Primer for Neighborhood Planning*, New York, Revere Copper and Brass, Inc., 1944.

"A Dairy Farm," *Beaux-Arts Institute of Design Bulletin*, XXV (March 1949), pp. 2–5.

"Toward a Plan for Midtown Philadelphia," *Perspecta, The Yale Architectural Journal*, II (1953), pp. 10–27.

"On the Responsibility of the Architect," discussion, *Perspecta, The Yale Architectural Journal*, II (1953), pp. 45–57.

Statements by Kahn in *Architecture and the University*. Proceedings of a conference held at Princeton University, December 11–12, 1953. Princeton, N.J., The School of Architecture, Princeton University, 1954. (See especially pp. 27, 29, 67–8.)

"Order and Design," *Perspecta, The Yale Architectural Journal*, III (1955), p. 59.

"Two Houses," *Perspecta, The Yale Architectural Journal*, III (1955), pp. 60–61. DeVore House; Adler House.

"A Synagogue: Adath Jeshurun of Philadelphia," *Perspecta, The Yale Architectural Journal*, III (1955), pp. 62–63.

"An Approach to Architectural Education," *Pennsylvania Triangle* (Philadelphia), XLII (Jan. 1956), pp. 28–32. City Tower; Statement by Robert Le Ricolais.

"Space, Form, Use," *Pennsylvania Triangle*, XLIII (Dec. 1956), pp. 43–47. Library, Washington University, St. Louis.

"Architecture Is the Thoughtful Making of Spaces. The Continual Renewal of Architecture Comes from Changing Concepts of Space," *Perspecta, The Yale Architectural Journal*, IV (1957), pp. 2–3; "Order in Architecture," pp. 58–65.

"The Entrance to a Theater," *National Institute for Architectural Education Bulletin*, XXXIII (Jan. 1957), pp. 22–23.

"Spaces, Order, and Architecture," *Royal Architectural Institute of Canada Journal*, XXXIV (Oct. 1957), pp. 375–77.

"On Philosophical Horizons," *A.I.A. Journal*, XXXIII (June 1960), pp. 99–100.

"World Design Conference," *Industrial Design*, VII (July 1960), pp. 46–49. Statement by Louis Kahn, p. 49.

"Marin City Redevelopment," *Progressive Architecture*, XLI (Nov. 1960), pp. 149–53. Critique by Kahn, p. 151.

"A Statement," *Arts and Architecture*, LXXVIII (Feb. 1961), pp. 14–15, 30.

"Form and Design," *Architectural Design*, XXXI (April 1961), pp. 145–54. This paper was recorded for the Voice of America Forum Series, 1960.

"Architecture—Fitting and Befitting: the new art of urban design—are we equipped?" *Architectural Forum*, CXIV (June 1961), p. 88.

"Louis Kahn," discussion, *Perspecta, The Yale Architectural Journal*, VII (1961), pp. 9–28. Goldenberg House, Rydal, Pa.; U.S. Consulate, Luanda, Portuguese Angola; First Unitarian Church, Rochester, N.Y.

A transcript of Kahn's talk at the conclusion of the C.I.A.M. Congress, Otterlo, Holland, September, 1959; in Oscar Newman, *New Frontiers in Architecture*, New York, 1961, pp. 205–16.

"Education for Urban Design, part I: The Changing Role of the Architect," *Journal of Architectural Education*, XVI (Autumn 1961), published as a part of *A.I.A. Journal*, XXXVI (Dec. 1961), pp. 85–104. The 1961 A.I.A.-A.S.C.A.

Ross Dixon, "Coffee Break with Louis I. Kahn—A Very Modern Architect,"
Philadelphia Sunday Bulletin Magazine (Jan. 28, 1962), p. 12.

CHRONOLOGICAL LIST OF ARTICLES

ON KAHN'S PROJECTS AND COMPLETED WORKS

Carl A. Ziegler, "The Sesqui-Centennial Exposition in Philadelphia," *American Architect*, CXXI (1922), pp. 382–85. See entry below under John Molitor.

"First Preliminary Competition for 17th Paris Prize, Society of Beaux-Arts Architects. A Monumental Entrance to a Thoroughfare," *American Architect*, CXXV (1924), p. 210. Student project, University of Pennsylvania; placed fifth, first mention.

"Class 'A'—III Project—A Shopping Center. Student Work, Beaux-Arts Institute of Design," *American Architect*, CXXV (1924), p. 366. Student project, University of Pennsylvania; second medal.

"Second Preliminary Competition for 17th Paris Prize, Society of Beaux-Arts Architects. A United States Veterans' Hospital," *American Architect*, CXXV (1924), p. 446. Student project, University of Pennsylvania; placed sixth (first alternate), first mention.

"Class 'A'—V Project—An Army Post. Student Work, Beaux-Arts Institute of Design," *American Architect*, CXXVI (1924), p. 297. Student project, University of Pennsylvania; second medal.

John Molitor, "How the Sesqui-Centennial Was Designed," *American Architect*, CXXX (1926), pp. 377–82. Does not mention Kahn, who states that he was " 'Chief of Design' in charge of all drafting and design for all exposition buildings."

The Housing Projects done by Architectural Research Group were published in: *Philadelphia Inquirer*, April 23, 1933; *Philadelphia Record*, April 23, 1933; *Philadelphia Inquirer*, April 30, 1933, *Philadelphia Record*, May 14, 1934.

"Imaginative Study of Philadelphia Done Over on Modernistic Planning Principles," *Philadelphia Evening Bulletin*, May 17, 1941, p. 3.

"Defense Housing at Middletown, Pa., George Howe and Louis I. Kahn, Associated Architects," *Architectural Forum*, CXXV (October 1941), pp. 216–17.

"450 Permanent Units—Rental. Middletown, Pa.," *Architectural Forum*, LXXVI (May 1942), pp. 306–7. George Howe and Louis I. Kahn, associated architects.

George Howe, Oscar Stonorov and Louis I. Kahn, " 'Standards' versus Essential Space: comments on unit plans for war housing," *Architectural Forum*, LXXVI (May 1942), pp. 307–11.

"The Town of Willow Run, Neighborhood Unit 3, Stonorov and Kahn, Architects," *Architectural Forum*, LXXVIII (March 1943), pp. 52–54.

"New Buildings for 194X: Hotel," *Architectural Forum*, LXXVIII (May 1943), pp. 74–79. Oscar Stonorov and Louis I. Kahn, architects.

"U.S. Wartime Housing," *Architectural Review*, XCVI (August 1944), pp. 29–58. See specifically pp. 33, 41, 44, 46, 48, 51.

"Carver Court, Coatesville, Pa.," *Architectural Forum*, LXXXI (Dec. 1944), pp. 109–16. Howe, Stonorov, Kahn, designers; Stonorov and Kahn, architects.

"You and Your Neighborhood . . . A Primer," Review, *Architectural Forum*, LXXXII (Jan. 1945), p. 150. Review of publication by Stonorov and Kahn.

"House in Melrose Park, Pennsylvania Provides Spaciousness in a Compact Plan," *Architectural Forum*, LXXXIII (Aug. 1945), pp. 132–34. Jessie Oser House.

"Postwar Construction, Portfolio of Philadelphia Architects No. 1, The Office of Stonorov and Kahn, Associated Architects of the A.I.A.," *Philadelphia*, XXXIII, No. 9 (Sept. 1945), pp. 23–27.

"Pine Ford Acres, Pa.," *Architectural Forum*, LXXXIV (Jan. 1946), pp. 110–11. Second community buildings. George Howe, Louis I. Kahn, architects.

"Philadelphia Psychiatric Hospital, Philadelphia, Pa.," *Progressive Architecture*, XXVII (Nov. 1946), pp. 81–88. Oscar Stonorov and Louis I. Kahn, architects. Isadore Rosenfield, hospital consultant.

"Student Architects, Painters, Sculptors Design Together," *Progressive Architecture*, XXX (May 1949), pp. 14, 16, 18.

"Glass Front Store in Philadelphia," *Architectural Forum*, XCI (Dec. 1949), pp. 94–95. Coward Shoe Store, Philadelphia. Oscar Stonorov and Louis I. Kahn, associated architects.

"Behind the Blueprints: Louis Kahn," *Architectural Forum*, XCIII (Sept. 1950), p. 79.

"Modern Space Framed with Traditional Artistry," *Architectural Forum*, XCIII (Sept. 1950), pp. 100–5. Weiss House, Morristown, Pa. Louis I. Kahn, architect.

"Mental Hospital," *Architectural Forum*, XCV (Sept. 1951), pp. 198–200. Philadelphia Psychiatric Hospital. Recreation and Occupational Therapy Wing. Louis I. Kahn, architect. Isadore Rosenfield, hospital consultant.

"The Philadelphia Cure: clearing slums with penicillin, not surgery," *Architectural Forum*, XCVI (April 1952), pp. 112–19.

"Tetrahedral Floor System: Yale's new design laboratory conceals lighting and ductwork within a 31 inch deep floor structure," *Architectural Forum*, XCVII (November 1952), pp. 148–49. Douglas Orr and Louis I. Kahn, associated architects. H. A. Pfisterer, structural engineer.

"New Hospital Type Brings the Spark of Good Architecture to the Mentally Ill, Substitutes Glass for Bars," *Architectural Forum*, XCVIII (Jan. 1953), pp. 118–21. Philadelphia Psychiatric Hospital. Samuel Radbill Building. Louis I. Kahn, architect. Isadore Rosenfield, hospital consultant.

A.I.A. Journal, XIX (June 1953), p. 267. Made Fellow of American Institute of Architects.

"P/A Views," *Progressive Architecture*, XXXV (May 1954), pp. 15–16, 22, 24. Letters to the Editor about the Yale Art Gallery from Robert W. McLaughlin, Leopold Arnaud, H. Holmes Perkins, Frederick Gutheim, José Luis Sert, C. Clark Macomber.

George A. Sanderson, "Extension: University Art Gallery and Design Center," *Progressive Architecture*, XXXV (May 1954), pp. 88–101; 130–31. Douglas Orr and Louis I. Kahn, associated architects.

"Spatial Triangulation, City Hall, Philadelphia, Pa.," *Progressive Architecture*, XXXV (June 1954), p. 102.

Boris Pushkarev, "Yale University Art Gallery and Design Center," *Perspecta, The Yale Architectural Journal*, III (1955), pp. 46–59.

Vincent Scully, Jr., "Le Musée des Beaux-Arts de l'Université Yale, New Haven," *Museum* (UNESCO), IX (1956), pp. 101–9 (French text); pp. 110–13 (English text).

"The Record Reports: Murphy and Mackey Design Wins Washington University Competition," *Architectural Record*, CXX (July 1956), p. 16.

"P/A News Survey: St. Louis Architects Win Washington University Competition," *Progressive Architecture*, XXXVII (July 1956), pp. 76–77.

A City Tower: a concept of natural growth. Universal Atlas Cement Company, United States Steel Corporation Publication No. ADUAC–707–57 (5–BM–WP), 1957.

Ian McCallum, ed., "Genetrix: Personal Contributions to American Architecture; Louis Kahn," *Architectural Review*, CXXI (May 1957), pp. 34–45.

Walter McQuade, "Architect Louis Kahn and His Strong-Boned Structures," *Architectural Forum*, CVII (Oct. 1957), pp. 134–43. A Russian language version was published in *America Illustrated*, No. 48, pp. 21–23, by the U.S.I.A. for distribution in the Soviet Union (courtesy of *Architectural Forum*).

"Louis Kahn and the Living City," *Architectural Forum*, CVIII (Mar. 1958), pp. 114–19.

"Logic and Art in Precast Concrete: Medical Research Laboratory, University of Pennsylvania, Philadelphia, Pa.," *Architectural Record*, CXXXVI (Sept. 1959), pp. 232–38.

Henry-Russell Hitchcock, "Notes of a Traveller: Wright and Kahn," *Zodiac*, VI (1960), pp. 14–21. Guggenheim Museum and the Richards Building.

Alison and Peter Smithson, "Louis Kahn," *Architects' Yearbook*, IX (1960), pp. 102–18. Sketch of Siena, Carver Court, Richards Medical Research Building, Weiss House, Philadelphia planning schemes, City Tower, Yale Art Gallery, DeVore House, Goldenberg House, Fleisher House, Morris House.

"Louis Kahn Honored," *Architectural Record*, CXXVII (May 1960), p. 25. National Institute of Arts and Letters, Arnold W. Brunner Award.

"People in the Arts," *Arts*, XXXIV (May 1960), p. 12. Kahn receives Brunner Award.

Alison Smithson, ed., "CIAM, Team 10," *Architectural Design*, XXX (May 1960), pp. 192–93. The work of invited participants: Louis Kahn.

"A Text Piece for Younger Architects," *Pennsylvania Gazette* (Alumni Magazine, University of Pennsylvania), LIX (June 1960), p. 15.

"Kahn's Medical Science Building Dedicated at University of Pennsylvania," *Progressive Architecture*, XXXXI (June 1960), p. 61.

Hiroki Onobayashi, "Louis Kahn: Order for Concrete," *Kokusai Kentiku*, XXVII (June 1960), pp. 49–53.

"Form Evokes Function," *Time*, LXXV (June 6, 1960), p. 76.

James Marston Fitch, "A Building of Rugged Fundamentals," *Architectural Forum*, CXIII (July 1960), pp. 82–87, 185. Richards Medical Research Building.

F. Tentori, "Ordine e Forma nell'opera di Louis Kahn," *Casabella*, No. 241 (July 1960), pp. 2–17.

"Art Serves Science: Alfred Newton Richards Medical Research Building, University of Pennsylvania, Philadelphia, Pa.," *Architectural Record*, CXXVIII (Aug. 1960), pp. 147–56.

"Louis I. Kahn's Blueprint for Revolution," *Greater Philadelphia Magazine*, LI (Sept. 1960), pp. 68–72.

"Louis Kahn, Laboratoires à l'Université de Pennsylvanie, États-Unis," *L'Architecture d'Aujourd'hui* (Paris), Nos. 91–92 (Sept.–Oct.–Nov. 1960), pp. 66–67.

" 'Arcaismo' Technologico," *L'Architettura* (Milan), VI (Oct. 1960), pp. 410–11. Richards Medical Research Building.

William H. Jordy, "Medical Research Building for Pennsylvania University, Philadelphia," *Architectural Review* (London), CXXIX (Feb. 1961), pp. 98–106.

Hiroki Onobayashi, "Louis Kahn and Alfred Newton Richards Medical Research Building," *Kokusai Kentiku*, XXVIII (Mar. 1961), pp. 64–69.

Jan C. Rowan, "Wanting To Be: The Philadelphia School," *Progressive Architecture*, XLII (April 1961), pp. 130–49. First Unitarian Church, Rochester, N.Y.; U.S. Consulate, Luanda, Portuguese Angola; Institute for Biology, Torrey Pines, California.

Wilder Green, "Louis I. Kahn, Architect: Alfred Newton Richards Medical Research Building, University of Pennsylvania, Philadelphia, 1958–60," *Museum of Modern Art Bulletin*, XXVIII, No. 1 (1961), pp. 1–24.

Ada Louise Huxtable, "In Philadelphia, an Architect," *New York Times*, June 11, 1961, II, p. 14, col. 3.

Wilder Green, "Medical Research Buildings—Louis Kahn," *Arts and Architecture*, LXXVIII (July 1961), pp. 14–17, 28. Reprint of text in *Museum of Modern Art Bulletin*, XXVIII, No. 1, 1961.

"Shapes of Tomorrow, Two Buildings in Diverging Directions," *Interiors*, CXX (July, 1961), p. 41. Louis I. Kahn: Richards Medical Research Building; Paul Rudolph: Galaxon Space Park.

"Richards Medical Research Building," *Arts*, XXXV (Sept. 1961), p. 66.

Enzo Fratelli, "Louis Kahn," *Zodiac*, VIII (1961), pp. 14–17. Reprint of "Order and Design," from *Perspecta, 3*; City Hall Project; a synagogue (Adath Jeshurun of Philadelphia); Richards Medical Research Building; Trenton Bath House.

Ueli Roth, "Louis Kahn und die Medical Towers in Philadelphia," *Werk*, XLIX (Jan. 1962), pp. 22–25.

"Laboratoires de Recherches Alfred Newton," *Aujourd'hui, Art et Architecture*, XXXV (Feb. 1962), pp. 1, 76–81.

Mary Harrington Hall, "Gifts from the Sea and the High Hopes of Jonas Salk," *San Diego Magazine*, XIV (Feb. 1962), pp. 41–45, 105–6.

Don West, "Doctor Salk's Bold New Venture," *Pageant Magazine*, XVII (Feb. 1962), pp. 156–61.

Rayner Banham, "Louis I. Kahn on Trial: The Buttery-Hatch Aesthetic," *Architectural Review*, CXXXI (Mar. 1962), pp. 203–5. This article, as its curious title indicates, is intended as an attack upon the "servant-served" solutions of the Richards Building. Some of its points are well taken; others have already been answered in this text, as has, I hope, its general denunciation of Kahn's "Form-Design" semantics.

"The Man Behind Mikveh Israel's New Building," *The Jewish Exponent,* Philadelphia (March 30, 1962), p. 21.

CHRONOLOGICAL LIST OF WORKS DEALING WITH KAHN'S CAREER IN GENERAL CONTEXT

Elizabeth Mock, ed., *Built in U.S.A., 1932–1944.* New York, 1944. See pp. 66–67. Carver Court, Coatesville, Pa., 1944. Howe, Stonorov and Kahn, architects.

Art in Progress, a survey . . . New York, Museum of Modern Art, 1944. See p. 186. Carver Court, Coatesville, Pa., Howe, Stonorov and Kahn, architects.

Vincent Scully, Jr., "Archetype and Order in Recent American Architecture," *Art in America,* XLII (Dec. 1954), pp. 250–61. Hadrian's Villa, Johnson, Schweikher, Kahn, etc.

Reyner Banham, "The New Brutalism," *Architectural Review,* CXVIII (Dec. 1955), pp. 355–61.

Edmund N. Bacon, "Urban Designs of Today: Philadelphia," *Progressive Architecture,* XXXVII (Aug. 1956), pp. 108–9. Mill Creek Redevelopment Area.

Frederick Gutheim, "Philadelphia's Redevelopment," *Architectural Forum,* CV (Dec. 1956), pp. 128–36. Greenways plan; Mill Creek apartments.

James Reichley, "Philadelphia Does It: The Battle for Penn Center," *Harper's Magazine,* CCXIV (Feb. 1957), pp. 49–56.

Ian McCallum, *Architecture U.S.A.,* London, 1959, pp. 83–88.

Vincent Scully, Jr., "Modern Architecture at Yale," *The Yale Class Book,* 1960, pp. 254–72; *The Yale Banner,* CXIX (1960), pp. 206–24.

Philip Johnson, "Great Reputations in the Making: Three Architects," *Art in America,* XLVIII (Spring 1960), pp. 70–75. Discusses Louis Kahn, Paul Rudolph, Frederick Kiesler.

Vincent Scully, Jr., "The Precisionist Strain in American Architecture," *Art in America,* XLVIII (Summer 1960), pp. 46–53.

Cranston Jones, *Architecture Today and Tomorrow,* New York, 1961. See Chapter 18, "Louis Kahn: The Esthetic of Space."

Vincent Scully, Jr., *Modern Architecture,* New York, 1961.

———, "The Heritage of Wright," *Zodiac,* VIII (1961), pp. 8–13. Recorded for Voice of America Forum Lectures, September 1960.

George B. Tatum, *Penn's Great Town,* Philadelphia, University of Pennsylvania Press, 1961.

Peter Collins, "The Form-Givers," *Perspecta, The Yale Architectural Journal,* VII (1961), pp. 91–96.

James Gowan, "Notes on American Architecture," *ibid.,* pp. 77–82.

Walter McQuade, "The Exploded Landscape," *ibid.,* pp. 83–90.

Sibyl Moholy-Nagy, "The Future of the Past," *ibid.,* pp. 65–76.

Colin St. John Wilson, "Open and Closed," *ibid.,* pp. 92–102.

Donald Leslie Johnson, "Form and Architecture," *Progressive Architecture,* XLII (June 1961), pp. 168–70.

"Visionary Architecture and a One-Man Show at the Museum of Modern Art," *Progressive Architecture,* XLII (July 1961), p. 48.

Robin Boyd, "The New Vision in Architecture," *Harper's Magazine,* CCXXIII (July 1961), pp. 72–81.

Peter Blake, "Are You Illiterate About Modern Architecture?" *Vogue,* CXXXVIII (Sept. 15, 1961), pp. 180–81, 214, 218.

Vincent Scully, Jr., "Wright, International Style, and Kahn," *Arts* (Mar. 1962), pp. 67–71, 77. An abridged version of a talk, "Frank Lloyd Wright and Twentieth-Century Style," given at the Twentieth International Congress of the History of Art, New York, September, 1961, and to be published in full in the Acts of the Congress by the Princeton University Press, 1963.

PUBLICATIONS USED BY KAHN OR MENTIONED IN THE TEXT

Giovanni Battista Piranesi, *Il Campo Marzo dell' antica Roma, opera di G. B. Piranesi, socio della Real società degli antiquari di Londra,* Rome, 1762(?) Dedicated to Robert Adam.

Paul Letarouilly, *Édifices de Rome Moderne*, Paris, 1840.

———, *Plan Typographique de Rome Moderne*, Paris, 1841.

Eugène Emmanuel Viollet-le-Duc, *Dictionnaire Raisonné de l'Architecture Française du XIe au XVIe siècle*, 6 vols., Paris, 1854–68. Part of this was translated as *Rational Building* by George Martin Huss, New York, 1895.

———, *Entretiens sur l'Architecture*, 2 vols., Paris, 1863–72; trans. by Benjamin Bucknall as *Lectures on Architecture*, Boston, 1877–81.

———, *La Cité de Carcassonne*, Paris, 1878; trans. by Benjamin Bucknall as *Annals of a Fortress*, Bucknall, Boston, 1876.

David MacGibbon and Thomas Ross, *The Castellated and Domestic Architecture of Scotland*, 5 vols., Edinburgh, 1887; esp. I, p. 238.

Charles H. Moore, *Development and Character of Gothic Architecture*, London and New York, 1890.

Auguste Choisy, *Histoire de l'Architecture*, Paris, 1899. We are indebted to Reyner Banham, in his *Theory and Design in the First Machine Age*, New York, 1960, for insisting upon the general significance of Choisy in modern architectural theory. A related theme has been treated by Robert Stern in his article on George Howe's academic background, "P.S.F.S.: Beaux-Arts Theory and Rational Expressionism," to be published in the *Journal of the Society of Architectural Historians* in 1962, along with William Jordy's discussion of the same building as a monument of the International Style.

Julien Guadet, *Éléments et Théorie de l'Architecture*, Paris, 1902.

Hector d'Espouy, *Fragments d'Architecture Antique*, Paris, 1905.

Charles H. Moore, *Character of Renaissance Architecture*, London and New York, 1905.

Charles Edouard Jeanneret-Gris (Le Corbusier), *Vers Une Architecture*, Paris, 1923; trans. by Frederick Etchells as *Towards a New Architecture*, London, 1927.

———, *Oeuvre Complète*, Zurich, 1929—.

T-Square Club Journal, published in Philadelphia, December 1930–December 1931; became *T-Square*, January 1932; became *Shelter* April 1932–November 1932. *Shelter* was reactivated and published in New York, March 1938–April 1939.

José Ortiz Echaque, *España Castillos y Alcazares*, Publicaciones Ortiz-Echaque, Madrid, 1956.

Perspecta, The Yale Architectural Journal, New Haven, Conn., School of Art and Architecture, Yale University, II (1953), III (1955), IV (1957), VII (1961).

Illustration Credits

Unless otherwise noted, all illustrations are courtesy of the office of Louis I. Kahn

Alinari Photo, Florence: 24
American Architect, CXXV (1924) : 7, CXXX (1926) : 8
Architectural Forum, XC (1950) : 16
Architecture, LXIII (1931) : 9
Ashbee, C. R., *Frank Lloyd Wright: Ausgeführte Bauten* (Berlin, 1911) : 54, 87
Cartier-Bresson, Henri, Magnum: Frontispiece
Chicago Architectural Photographing Company: 86
Choisy, Auguste, *Histoire de l'Architecture* (Paris, 1899) : 5, 6
Cleff, Bernie, Philadelphia: 59
Condax, John, Philadelphia: 103
Cook, James, Pittsburgh: 78, 79, 80, 81
Damora, Robert, Bedford Village, N.Y.: 62
Ebstel, John, New York City: 17A, 17B, 18, 20, 36, 45, 46, 49, 50, 51, 71
Engdahl, Bill, Hedrich-Blessing, Chicago: 26
Freedman, Lionel, New York City: 30A, 30B, 35, 37, 38
Hervé, Lucien, Paris: 28, 29
Hitchcock, Henry-Russell, *In the Nature of Materials: The Buildings of Frank Lloyd Wright* (New York, 1942) : 52
Hubbard, Cortlandt V. D., Philadelphia: 19, 39
MacGibbon and Ross, *The Castellated and Domestic Architecture of Scotland* (Edinburgh, 1887–92) : 116
Courtesy of the Massachusetts Institute of Technology: 27
Matter, Herbert, New York City: 34
Meyers, Marshall D., Philadelphia: 12, 67, 77, 82, 84A, 84B, 84C, 85, 92, 95, 96, 98A, 98B, 115, 125
Molitor, Joseph W., Ossining, New York: 73
Courtesy of the Museum of Modern Art, New York: 2, 11, 65, 74, 75, 76
Perspecta, 2 (1953) : 60, 121; 3 (1955) : 33, 40, 42, 43, 44; 4 (1957) : 61, 63B, 63C, 122; 7 (1961) : 89, 90, 91
Pohl, George, Philadelphia: 105, 106, 107, 109, 112, 113, 126
Porter, William L., Philadelphia: 88, 94
Regional Planning Federation of the Philadelphia Tri-State District (Philadelphia, 1932) : 3
Robinson, Cervin, New York City: 68
Schmertz, Mildred, New York City: 72
Smith, Malcolm/Architectural Graphics Associates, Wilton, Conn.: 69, 70
Universal Atlas Cement Company: 63A
Viollet-le-Duc, *La Cité de Carcassonne* (Paris, 1878) : 127
Wells, John R., Philadelphia: 4
Courtesy of the Frank Lloyd Wright Foundation: 52
Courtesy of the Yale University Art Library Photographic Collection: 10, 25

Text printed in offset by Murray Printing Company, Forge Village, Massachusetts; illustrations in Pictone offset by Pictorial Offset, New York City. Set in Bodoni Book with Inserat Grotesk. Bound by The Haddon Craftsmen, Scranton, Pennsylvania. Format by Lustig & Reich.

46899

NA
737
K32
S38

SCULLY, VINCENT
LOUIS I. KAHN.